Praise for *Your Good Work Habits Toolbox*

"I was introduced to Beck while watching MSNBC's Squawk Box in 2016 at the very dawn of the emerging field of virtual reality. That day I found myself driven to meet this extraordinary entrepreneur. In the years since, I've watched Beck develop and share his *Good Work Habits Toolbox*. Today I often ask aspiring founders to spend time with Beck for his counsel. Everyone will take something from this book. A careful read will help you and others achieve personal and company goals. Enjoy!"

— Lee Arnold, executive chair, Colliers International;
CEO, LA Financial; venture investor

"I wish I had this book on day one of my professional career. I would have avoided costly mistakes, advanced my career faster, and been better positioned for future success in life. The lessons that Beck has taught me over the years have allowed me to excel both professionally and personally. Beck's decades of building successful businesses and thriving teams provides trusted practical advice for both the seasoned business professional and those just starting in their careers.

—Jessi Sparks, vice president of strategy, Magnetic Mobile

"If you are lucky, you'll have the opportunity to work for someone who will take you on a life-changing professional journey. Beck has been that person for me. He is both a student and an artist in life and in leadership, an authentic and uncommon leader whose satisfaction comes from watching the people around him succeed."

—Sonia Schechter, CMO Marxent

an imprint of Amplify | Publishing Group

www.amplifypublishing.com

Your Good Work Habits Toolbox: Crafting the Skills Now That Will
Transform Your Career and Elevate Your Organizational Value

For more information, please contact:
Amplify Publishing, an imprint of Amplify Publishing Group
620 Herndon Parkway, Suite 320
Herndon, VA 20170
info@amplifypublishing.com

Library of Congress Control Number: 2022908934

CPSIA Code: PRV1122A

ISBN-13: 978-1-64543-733-8

Printed in the United States

To my boys, Alex and Gabe. I'm looking forward to watching your personal and professional journeys. I hope that we get to break down business models together and that you let me invest in your great ideas. I had the opportunity to have a professional life that saw the invention of the internet, mobile phones, electric cars, and even the metaverse. I hope your generation gets to experience the same kind of transformation and that you find this book useful.

To Barry, my adventure brother. From our first go-karts and tree houses to the many years we've spent in business together, nobody could ask for a better partner. Thank you.

To all the wonderful team members and mentors with whom I've had the opportunity to go to battle over the years. Thank you for your support and guidance.

To Camelia, my wife. I've asked way too much of you. I've worked way too many hours. I've talked your ear off repeatedly. I love you. Thank you for all your support and love. You've been my mentor in what it means to care, love, and provide for others.

Special thanks to David Hillman for providing the illustrations.

Your GOOD WORK HABITS *TOOLBOX*

Crafting the Skills Now That Will Transform Your Career and Elevate Your Organizational Value

BECK BESECKER

an imprint of Amplify Publishing Group

TABLE OF CONTENTS

CHAPTER 3: GOOD PEOPLE HABITS...............95

CHAPTER 4: GOOD CULTURE HABITS...............125

FOREWORD

BECK AND I HAVE forged similar career paths, from launching ventures at the dawn of the Internet to building multiple tech businesses that would change consumer engagement forever.

But as long as I've known Beck, he's been obsessed with how to help others advance in their careers. "Success isn't real unless shared" is more than a tenant he'll impart, it's a mantra he lives by.

In *Your Good Work Habits Toolbox*, Beck has taken aim at teaching lessons and frameworks that we don't learn in college and might take years to accumulate on the job. It's quintessential Beck. He doesn't care about fancy-sounding jargon. He gets down to what counts. He focuses on what works. And he does it with heart.

Beck has organized his advice into a fun and easy-to-read framework that covers good personal-process habits, good communication, and good people habits.

If you're fresh out of college looking to make a great first impression in your first professional job, Beck's toolbox will help you unlock how to get ahead.

If you've advanced in your career and you have to learn a new role, Beck's toolbox will help you charge forward with confidence.

If you're struggling in your current role and frustrated with poor working relationships, Beck's toolbox will help you build a new perspective that can right the ship and build great relationships with your teammates and boss.

You'll learn how to develop good judgment and make faster decisions, respond like a pro, advance a project more quickly, build better teams, steer clear of toxic team members, and more. You'll also learn the secret to giving better presentations. And finally, for aspiring leaders who have mastered great habits, you'll learn the principles of building a strong team culture.

Beck's book comes at a time when good work habits are more important than ever. For many of us, learning these habits is even more challenging without a physical workplace and the informal relationships that lead to learning, mentorship, and camaraderie. If you're new to a job and you're working partially or entirely from home, Beck's toolbox is a must read.

We need more bosses, executives, and influential businesspeople who subscribe to Beck's view of leadership and how to treat people in the ever-evolving workplace. Thanks to Your Good Work Habits Toolbox, many emerging leaders will have that opportunity.

Josh Linkner
Five-time tech entrepreneur, *New York Times* bestselling author of *Big Little Breakthroughs*, venture capitalist

INTRODUCTION
THE EMPTY TOOLBOX

10980 CIRCLE HILL ROAD, *Pleasant Hill, Ohio.* Twenty-two acres of corn, soybeans, and tobacco next to our neighbor's acreage of corn, soybeans, and tobacco, next to his neighbor's acreage of corn, soybeans, and tobacco, and so on and so on, for miles and miles. We grew up on that little patch of farmland in the middle of thousands of light green and dark green postage-stamp plots that you see when you fly over the Midwest. The only distinct landmark that broke up the repeating pattern was a small tributary of the Stillwater River called Panther Creek. The river, I imagined, was once a raging force at some point in its journey, but it waned to a meandering brook of no more than fifteen yards across as it passed near our farm.

My brother and I stood knee-deep in Panther Creek for much of our childhood catching crawdads. Our many adventures included hunting arrowheads, chasing cows, learning to fish, and peeing on our neighbor's electric fence. Just us for miles. Of course, our parents taught us a lot on the farm and in life, but here, at that creek, we were on our own, like two feral animals honing our skills through trial, error, and skinned knees. We were fiercely independent and self-sufficient.

My brother, Barry, and I loved to learn by doing—building, tearing down, building again, and celebrating each go-kart, parachute, tree house, zip line, and raft along the way. I know that our business life together has been a bit of a grown-up version of what we did together as kids—building something cool so we can celebrate with high fives and red Kool-Aid. Raw curiosity and learning-though-doing is an incredibly effective way to grow.

But it's not enough.

In school, we learn the fundamentals that we'll use in our chosen careers. A variety of activities—including sports, scouting, volunteering, and clubs—teach us about working as a team toward a common goal.

Yet, there is still another set of skills everyone must learn to have a successful and rewarding career. I think of it as an empty toolbox that is your responsibility to fill with the knowledge and skills you won't learn in school and formal activities.

This "toolbox" is not as obviously useful and doesn't have a designated institution of learning or syllabus. But believe me, this skill set is just as important to your career as your public school or Ivy League education. I have a simple name for it: *good work habits.*

I've always thought it odd that schools don't teach many of the skills that are fundamental to everyday living. For instance, it's rare to find personal finance taught in high school, while it's obvious that saving early in life and avoiding unnecessary debt are basic financial skills that will have tremendous impact on everyone's quality of life. Alongside personal finance, basic good work habits are another topic that high schools and colleges fail to impart.

What are good work habits? In short, they are personal systems we all need to navigate the workplace—tools, techniques, and frameworks that we can use to organize ourselves, to communicate effectively, and to work well with others. You can learn many good work habits through trial and error, like we did by sinking raft after raft in Panther Creek. Others you'll learn by emulating a boss or peer.

If you're really lucky, you'll find mentors that will teach you good work habits. Mentors are by far the most effective way to learn good work habits for two reasons. One, they can fast-track your learning by sharing their own experiences. And two, mentors will impart advice even when you didn't know you needed it. For my money, that is what real mentorship is about—sharing hard truths that aren't always easy to hear.

Unfortunately, many people struggle in their careers because they never learn to consistently employ good work habits; they don't fully understand why it's been so difficult to get that next promotion, get along with colleagues, or reach their goals.

For me, it took much too long to learn that "feedback is love." Anyone who has spent any amount of time with me has heard me utter these three words. It has become one of my favorite work habits. Taking positive reinforcement is easy. But being critiqued sucks. We *all* take it personally. Nobody "takes feedback well" . . . even if someone says they do.

It always makes me crack a smile when a job candidate says, "I really love constructive feedback." There is one very simple truth about critical feedback to keep in mind: if someone takes the time to give it to you (even if not delivered in the most caring and eloquent way), it means *you* are worth the investment. You shouldn't worry when you get tough feedback; you should start to worry when they stop giving it to you! Much more on taking and giving feedback lies ahead in these pages.

Filling Your Toolbox: Good Personal-Process, Communication, and People Habits

This book is a collection of good work habits that I've learned from coworkers, bosses, and mentors throughout my career. It's a toolbox, if you will. Not unlike the various drill bits, wrenches, screwdrivers, and specialized machines a woodworker accumulates over the years, you'll find some pieces of advice that are perpetually useful. Others you may only use once every few years, but they are the perfect tools for certain jobs. Regardless of how frequently you use them, you know just where to look when you need guidance. Your toolbox and mine won't and don't need to look exactly the same, but collecting and referencing a reliable toolbox can be an invaluable asset that will help you throughout your career.

The content of this book is organized into three main chapters: "Good Personal-Process Habits," "Good Communication Habits," and "Good People Habits." We'll introduce a number of topics in each section, share a few stories, have a few laughs, and then I'll leave you with tips and tools to use as you navigate your work world.

Working from Home: Good Work Habits Are Paramount

Working remotely is now a permanent component of how businesses operate. The opportunity to work off-site is among the most important variables that candidates consider in assessing a job opportunity, and it is one of the first questions they ask in interviews. Remote work is clearly here to stay.

The content of this book was collected over a ten-year period and originally appeared in a series of blog posts aimed at educating our team members at Marxent on good work habits. Much of this content was also repurposed into lessons that we teach in a series of employee training programs called "Empower Hours." When COVID-19 hit and we all went remote, it became evident that the foundation we had built for good work habits became a system that helped us navigate this new reality.

In this new remote work world, good work habits are even more important to teach and reinforce, especially for employees who are brand new to the workforce. As noted, many good work habits are learned and developed by watching and mirroring others. This is obviously much more difficult to do without a physical work environment.

While the personal-process, communication, and people habits we'll explore here are timeless, our new remote work reality now makes them imperative for team members to learn and for companies to thrive. Given this new normal, we will discuss the implications for each habit for remote workers and teams in a sidebar as we explore each topic. We want to make sure your toolbox is ready for many years to come, and more than likely as a manager or employee, remote work will be an evolving environment you will continue to navigate.

I decided, in large part, to write this book based on living and working though COVID-19 over the past two years. It became very clear that team members with strong personal processes, good communication skills, and great people habits excelled. In fact, they became *more* productive once they were spending less time getting to and from work and weren't expected to travel. The popular sentiment among most leaders whom I spoke with in the early days of the pandemic was that productivity and accountability would suffer across the board. While this wasn't the case with team members who had a strong toolbox, it was in fact the case among team members who did not have well-formed work habits. Employees who were new to the workforce who had not yet had the opportunity to build their toolbox also struggled.

While teaching good work habits isn't part of a standard college curriculum today, I predict that the advent of working remotely will make it a heavily researched field going forward, and it will eventually become a part of the standard college education. Moreover, teaching good work habits will need to be built into standard business operations for remote teams to survive and thrive.

Building Strong Teams: Culture Habits

We'll explore good personal work habits in the first three chapters, then, in the final chapter, we'll discuss good "culture habits" that bond great teams. Once you've mastered good personal work habits, it's inevitable that you'll progress and have the opportunity to lead your own team or functional area—or perhaps even your own company.

As a leader, your single most important responsibility will be building a strong culture. Peter Drucker, renowned business writer, is often quoted as saying, "Culture eats strategy for breakfast." He's right, of course. It's impossible for us to be our best in a toxic or unmotivating work environment. But how do you create and maintain a great culture? This too is a discipline that isn't taught in school, is often misunderstood, and is not easily mastered. We'll use the final chapter to explore what I call good "culture habits" and a framework for building great teams. We'll also look at why good culture habits are now more important than ever.

CHAPTER 1
GOOD PERSONAL-PROCESS HABITS

IT'S NO SECRET THAT great athletes and musicians are disciplined people. Great organizations, teams, and employees are also disciplined. That is, greatness requires a repeatable set of processes or habits. For an athlete, a good personal process consists of practicing the fundamentals repeatedly, building strength and speed each day, and relentlessly studying a playbook. But what does a good personal process look like for great employees? While the fundamentals of your chosen career are taught in school, building a personal process as an employee is often a "learning on the job" exercise that you learn from a boss, from watching peers, or from a mentor.

Good companies have a strategic plan (e.g., what we are selling, where we are selling it, this makes us different, this is our vision for the future, etc.) and an operating plan (e.g., we need these resources, these are our goals for the next year, this is how we will measure success, etc.). Just like well-run companies, excellent employees also have an "operating system."

In this first chapter, we'll review work habits that you can incorporate into your personal process, including consistency, asking for help, prioritization, planning, updating and reporting, creating a good project scope, judgment and decision-making, the power of grit, and working in white space. Master these and you will be a valued employee, great teammate, and appreciated by your boss and team.

Your Personal-Process Toolbox

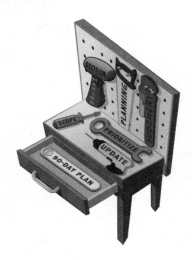

I want to start by sharing three key traits that you need to have in your toolbox as soon as possible: consistency, prioritizing, and asking for help. They are your starter kit for good work habits.

WHO NOTICES CONSISTENCY?

There is nothing better than working with a colleague who has their act together. That is, they have a consistent personal process for time management and a systematic, repeatable, and consistent method for managing tasks. A good personal process sends the message that an employee is on top of their game and is working toward meaningful deliverables and important dates. Moreover, when someone has a consistent personal process, it provides reassurance to management that important details won't slip through the cracks.

A good personal process is the *first* thing we look for in a prospective hire. During interviews, we'll often ask job candidates how they organize themselves. The wrong answer is: "The first thing I do when I get to the office is knock out email." Unfortunately, this is the answer I get all too often.

What does a good personal process look like? In golf, a player who lacks personal process will arrive late, head to the range, grab a bag of balls, select a club at random, and then hit balls here and there before heading off to the course. A player with an established personal process will work through their golf bag in a systematic way. She might hit each club in order, hit a specific number of balls at a specific target, or keep track of her success rate by club and distance.

Consistency is not flashy, and if it doesn't catch everybody's attention, just know that it gets the *right* people's attention. Simply put, it reduces the boss's stress and gets results. Consistency is a two-handed chest pass in a behind-the-back-bounce-pass world. Most people don't take note of the mundane or back-end work, but the ones who do notice are the ones you want to notice your work. Whom do you think they call on to handle the must-have account? Whom do they count on when initiating a new strategy or initiative?

A strong personal process can vary from person to person. There are no hard-and-fast rules. But there is one imperative: unwavering *consistency*. If your personal process is changing every week, it's not a process. Consistently reviewing lists and commitments on a good old yellow notepad is far more valuable than a pretty, multicolored spreadsheet that you look at once in a blue moon.

TACKLE THE HARD THINGS FIRST AND ASK FOR HELP EARLY

If you have a long list of to-dos and a limited time to get them done, always tackle the hard ones first. These are the tasks with the greatest number of unknowns, are the least defined, or are going to take time and concentration to complete. Too often, team members will work in the opposite direction, starting with the easy tasks so they can check things off the list. That may feel good, but it is often a recipe for disaster. Whether you have a big new customer launch, a new product to build, or new system to implement, always start off by identifying the biggest risks and biggest unknowns.

So how does this work in practice? Odds are your risky task isn't risky or unknown to someone else in your organization. That is, someone has probably done it before or can at least point you in the right direction. Nobody really expects you to know everything, especially if you're new to your job or role. Many employees fear that if they ask for direction, it will be seen as a sign of weakness. Nothing could be further from the truth. Your boss would *much* rather you ask for help early and often versus spinning your wheels trying to pretend that you have it all figured out. Hot tip: Your boss already knows you don't know everything. They are expecting you to need and ask for help. The worst-case scenario is that you don't ask for help and burn up the time you would have had to knock out your work.

PRIORITIZE LIKE A CEO

Most professionals not only juggle a lot of tasks, but they also have several areas of responsibility. While the purpose of this book isn't to train CEOs, the most extreme example of this is probably, in fact, the job of the CEO. Let's take a quick peek at how a CEO has to prioritize, as I think it's a good insight for you to have, then we'll look at how you might apply this discipline to your role.

A typical CEO is ultimately responsible for marketing, sales, product, finance, hiring, team development, client success, intellectual property, new business development, strategy, and planning, and so forth. But not all these responsibilities are of equal value to the organization, and of course, one can't get to everything all at one time. So how does a CEO decide where to spend their time first? There are probably multiple schools of thought here, but I always put sales first.

Why, you ask? Because if something doesn't get sold, nothing else in the business happens. My number-two focus is client success, because if clients are not successful, we're not getting paid, and if we lose a client, we're losing versus gaining ground. Next is team development, because if you don't have great leadership and a great team, it's hard to execute your strategy in the first place.

So how might prioritization look? Imagine a list of functions from left to right that starts with sales, customer success, and people, then is followed by product, marketing, finance, and so forth. While there will be leaders for each of these functions, odds are I'll need to provide input, direction, or resources or make decisions to contribute to these other functions, so I'll have a running list of tasks I need to get to at some point. But I've decided that if sales, customer success, or team functions need me, I'm always going to serve them first and make sure I get those responsibilities knocked out before I move to any other functions. If I just can't get to a lower priority function in a given day or week, that's a decision that I think is in the overall best interest of the company.

Now let's try this at the functional level. Let's imagine you're running marketing. Your responsibilities are likely to include events, public relations, product marketing, content creation, branding, advertising and lead generation, and so on. While all these are important responsibilities, they can't all be equally important. If they were, how would you know where to allocate your time effectively?

Ok, now imagine you're a member of the marketing team working under the chief marketing officer, and your job is advertising and lead generation. Your functional responsibilities are likely to include social media posts, paid media, creating SEO site content, event support, and perhaps helping with sales campaigns. Which of these functions are the best means of generating leads and where should you allocate your time? Prioritizing effectively requires that you weigh your responsibilities based on the value they create for the business. When tough choices need to be made about where resources and time are spent, this prioritizing should guide your decision-making.

In short, whether you're the CEO or an individual contributor, we all have to make choices as to where our efforts will make the greatest impact for your given organization. If you start thinking like a CEO, you realize they're not endowed with superpowers. You discover they are simply more experienced at handling and prioritizing multiple responsibilities and tasks, and they're good at not getting distracted by activities that are not important. If you're not sure which of your job functions are most important, collaborate with your boss or team. This is a great way to create agreement and get alignment.

REMOTE WORK AND . . . ASKING FOR HELP

Employees who are new to their organizations have been among the most impacted by working from home. While a good employee onboarding program should be standard, we found that during COVID-19 this type of program needed to be much more intentional. Here are several ways we now do just that:

- Ninety-day plans (which we'll cover later in this chapter) are now required for all new employees.
- All employees are required to participate in a review of the strategic plan.
- We assign each new employee a mentor.
- We invested heavily in a self-service training knowledge base.
- We give each employee a list of team members to meet and get to know in the first thirty days, most of whom will be outside their function. In effect, we are forcing interactions that would have probably occurred organically in a physical work environment.

Being of Two Minds: Planning vs. Execution

I like to imagine that I have two different people in my head—a general planning for battle and a soldier ready to take the field. But it's difficult to have both characters in my frontal lobe at the same time with one arguing which hill to take while the other is trying to make sure his rifle is loaded.

At the highest level, the month of November is when the general in my head is given the floor and we develop our strategic plan for the year. All our focus is on how we're positioned in the market, the strengths and weaknesses of our product, our positioning, capital requirements, and staffing needs. We build a detailed plan function by function that rolls up to a company vision and mission. By December 1 each year, we're ready to communicate the final plan to the team.

For the following year, we become soldiers working through our plan, except for those check-in points at the end of each month and quarter when the "general hat" is put back on to evaluate progress and adjust the plan. But what we're *not* doing is constantly rebuilding the plan. In software engineering it is popular to use SCRUM, a form of agile planning that locks down a plan in two- or three-week intervals. But no changes may be made to the plan during a "sprint." This same sort of "planning versus attacking" approach should also translate to your individual efforts, which means you need a system or habit.

My brother, Barry, has been my lifetime business partner. One of his favorite things to say is:

"IF YOU'RE WINGING IT, YOU'RE PROBABLY MARGINAL. IF YOU HAVE A PLAN, YOU'RE PROBABLY GOOD. BUT IF YOU HAVE A SYSTEM, YOU'RE GOING TO KICK ASS."

Barry is a computer science engineer, so "system thinking" comes very naturally to him. That is, why do something manually if you can simply write a routine? As a result, he's always looking beyond just a plan to creating a system that can be reliably and consistently repeated; contributors can easily come in and out of a defined system without too much effort. So how might a "planning versus doing" system look at the personal level?

I learned my personal "planning versus doing" from Chuck Wise, one of my first mentors. Chuck Wise (yes, Wise is really his name) was the senior VP of advancement at Purdue University. I met Chuck at an event while in graduate school, and he was the kind of person whose first inclination when he met you was to find out how he could help you. He was generous beyond measure. I was a poor graduate student. My bank account, unlike Chuck's generosity, was almost nonexistent. It was in the single digits . . . often. Chuck and I struck up a conversation, and by the end of it he was offering me a job in the Advancement Office to help with preparing the university for its first billion-dollar fundraising campaign. My job would be to help modernize the alumni and donor database in order to create a digital prospect management system. This job would sow the seeds of the next thirty years of my career, which would center around content management platforms.

I owe Chuck much, and I'll share many lessons I learned from "Mr. Wise" as we explore good work habits. Through him, I also had the opportunity to meet my childhood idol Neil Armstrong, the most famous Purdue grad. We'll save that story for later.

This role in the Advancement Office was the first time I'd ever worked on a project that involved several offices, many stakeholders, multiple technology vendors, and hundreds of contributors. And I was not at all qualified for the job. My saving grace was that all of this technology was relatively new at the time and nobody else was all that qualified either.

I felt a huge sense of responsibility, and it wasn't long before it was obvious that I was overwhelmed and poorly organized. Exasperated, I went to Chuck to air my frustrations and concerns, and he gave me counsel and direction that I've used every week of my life since. He shared: "Don't plan and execute at the same time."

The workweek is a whirlwind. There's way too much going on, too many meetings, and way too many Slacks coming in to concentrate and prioritize. I'm sure everyone feels this way. Once the week starts, it's off to the races. Chuck's advice was to build a system where you designate part of your time for *planning* and devote the rest of the week to *doing*. His system, which I borrowed with great effect, is to use Sunday evenings to plan the week. That way, when I wake up Monday morning, the soldier brain is ready to go with a clear set of objectives and tasks. The weeks where I skip Sunday night planning are always less productive. Moreover, I find that if I don't have a clear plan coming into the week, my anxiety is dramatically higher.

Vice versa, on Sundays I don't try and complete any work or get into the detail of any projects. I let my general brain have that time for only planning and prioritization. I also stole his habit of waking up early each morning to check the day's plan over a good espresso.

There are many more resources that you can consult about building a good personal process. *7 Habits of Highly Effective People* by Steven R. Covey is probably the most celebrated book on the topic and a must-read for anyone looking to boost their productivity.

While my personal process includes Sunday evening planning, your personal process can be unique to you and take any form you wish. What is critical is that (a) you adopt one and (b) that you use it consistently. Again, consistency is incredibly important. Because if you're consistent, it means you are reliable, which is another name for trustworthy. And if you're reliable, you're valuable. We'll talk about the value of consistency (i.e., the most powerful skill set in the world) throughout this book.

REMOTE WORK AND ... PRIORITIZATION

Developing a discipline and framework for personal prioritization becomes even more critical as we work from home. Many leaders prognosticated that an entirely remote workforce would lead to employees goofing off and reduced performance and productivity. On the whole, that didn't end up being the case for most organizations. But there were winners and losers. What we learned is that employees with strong personal processes thrived and became even more productive. They were able to recapture and put to use all of the hours spent driving to and from work . . . and probably a bit of time that was previously required to get out of their pajamas and take a shower. However, there were those who didn't make it in a remote work environment. And it was clear that all of these casualties had poor personal processes.

The Power of the 5x5: A Consistency Tool That Will Show Your Boss You Have Your Act Together

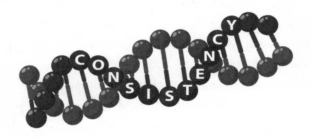

Assuming you've now built your personal process and you have your act together, how does your boss know it? She doesn't, unless you communicate it.

All of us have probably done some kind of home project like renovating a kitchen or something similar. Let's say you meet with the builder, set a schedule, kick off the project, and then . . . radio silence. Your builder doesn't send you updates; there's no list of what's going well or not. You have no idea what to expect or when the project will be done. One option is hope for the best and show up on the completion date and wait for the big reveal. Another option is to show up at the job site every day and ask questions until you get the answers you want. Both are terrible options. The first gives you no assurances your money is being well spent. The second option makes you an annoying micromanager.

A huge part of any team member's responsibility is active communication. And one of the simplest and most effective communication tools is the "5x5."

A 5x5 is a short email that takes no more than fifteen minutes to prepare. You send it every Friday at the end of the day to your boss and maybe a few other salient stakeholders. The email includes "five items completed this week" and "five priorities for next week." That's it. Literally, that's it. Super simple. Fifteen minutes a week and your boss never has to think, *What the heck is Bob doing this week?* I promise you: this super simple work habit can change your career.

At Marxent, all 120 employees complete a 5x5 and send it to me and their supervisor every week. It's part of what we call our "cultural habits"; these are habits that everyone does that reflect our shared values. If you're an aspiring leader, cultural habits are incredibly powerful. Again, we'll spend the last chapter of the book exploring these.

So, what does a good 5x5 look like? Here's an actual example from Valerie, who runs marketing production for us.

LAST WEEK:

- Reviewed Q1 project logistics with Sonia and Chris.
- Read about and researched e-commerce metrics.
- Finalized video scripts for remaining product videos and developed a new plan for 3D cloud and virtual reality videos. We will be planning a video shoot to gather

footage for both in Q1.

- Fleshed out a new product spotlight process with Chris.
- Quick shout out to Sonia for helping me with how to track LinkedIn metrics.

NEXT WEEK:

- Complete Q1 project timeline.
- Meet with Caroline to review inbound leads.
- Assist John and Jeff with the Developer Documentation project.
- Work with Chris on sprint demo presentation.
- Meet with the web developers to strategize for Q1.

WHY IS THE WEEKLY 5X5 SO POWERFUL? HERE ARE THE TOP REASONS:

- You're communicating that you have the "consistency gene," which engenders confidence and trust.
- You now have a regular line of communication that builds familiarity and comfort, which means the odds are better that you'll go to leadership with a challenging issue. That helps everybody.
- You can recognize the contributions of others that your leadership may not be privy to.
- Your leadership gets to say "thank you," and even provide coaching when needed.

Funny story. My editor for this book, Myles, left me a note in an early draft of the manuscript that asked, "Surely you don't read through them all. Do you randomly choose some to take a look at to get a sense of what's going on?" Yes, Myles, I read and respond to them all. I figure it takes me about fifteen to thirty seconds to read a 5x5. So, if my math is right, that's no more than an hour investment each week to learn, make a meaningful connection, and maybe provide some coaching or encouragement. I also get to learn about functions in the company where I have limited domain expertise, which makes me a smarter leader. More importantly, I get to say "thank you," which I'd argue is a pretty powerful leadership strategy. It costs nothing, takes little time, and tells team members they're appreciated. I don't know about you, but when someone thanks me for something, I always want to work harder and do more.

Sonia is our CMO at Marxent, and she taught me the power of the 5x5. I can't remember a single instance when I asked her for an update or when I didn't feel current on a project. Every time I get an update from her, I feel all warm and fuzzy inside and I say to myself, *She's got it under control. I can put my attention elsewhere.* If you can get *your* boss to think this about you, the world will be your oyster. So that's it. Weekly updates. You can read hundreds of books about how to get ahead in business, but I promise you this tiny, fifteen-minute discipline will tell your boss that you have your act together and will change your career.

REMOTE WORK AND . . . THE 5X5

Building close relationships is challenging to do when working remotely. There is real value in getting a sense of who someone is when you share the same physical space. We're all more than just who we are at work, and getting to know the outside interests of your coworkers and boss allows you to connect on shared interests as well as be empathetic when someone is going through a difficult personal situation. One of the organic things that happened when we went remote is that many employees started sharing parts of their personal lives in their 5x5s. Simple things like, "I'm off Friday, as we're taking the kids to Disney for a long weekend," or, "In personal news, my son is starting to look at where he wants to go to college," or, "Hey, you may not know, but Ellen's mom passed. She may not have shared that with you, but she is having a tough time right now." 5x5s became more than just a tool for effective communications; it became a tool to connect.

The Ninety-Day Plan: It's More Than Just a Probationary Period—It's a Way of Working

Want to make a great first impression in your new job? Feeling "stuck" and unable to make the impact you desire? Need a way to build credibility with your boss to ask for a raise? In all cases, building a ninety-day plan is a great tool to add to your good work habits toolbox.

The first ninety days of any job is crucial. It's the standard "grace period" for new employees and the time during which first impressions are made. But the value of the individual ninety-day plan extends far beyond starting a job—it's a way of life and a way of working. Most companies have an operating calendar. A strategic plan is built every year that includes annual goals and then goals by each quarter and month. Quarterly objectives will include revenue goals, cost goals, market goals, competitive objectives, product goals, and so forth. What does a good ninety-day plan look like for an employee? Here is a good and simple outline:

1. List your responsibilities.
2. Create a goal for each responsibility. A good goal will be SMART (specific, measurable, attainable, realistic, and time-bound). If you're not familiar with SMART goals, this is a broadly accepted standard for quality goal setting. Check it out.
3. Create an interim milestone at thirty days and sixty days that will show you're on or off track toward your ninety-day goals.

That's it. Pretty straightforward. Of course, your ninety-day plan should line up with your team and overall company objectives as well.

At a minimum, you should create a ninety-day plan when you start a new job or take on a new role. Odds are when you started a new job or role, you were given a job description. Sometimes, these job descriptions can be a little "boilerplate" and may or may not translate perfectly to your new responsibilities. Even if the job description is detailed and complete, it probably doesn't weigh or prioritize your list of responsibilities or outline what should be accomplished by when. A ninety-day plan can serve as a way to transform your list of responsibilities into an actionable plan that you can use to ensure that you have agreement with your boss on what needs to be done and in what order. I also find that just the process of transforming your new job responsibilities into a plan helps you cement and clarify your job in your own mind. This process also will drive conversation between you and your boss that will likely uncover any inconsistencies, conflicts, or lack of detail.

The following is an example of a ninety-day plan for a new hire. The first column is a list of responsibilities, and then the subsequent three columns can simply describe your progression against those responsibilities during each thirty-day window. This is the actual ninety-day plan for a new sales operations manager we recently hired.

Responsibility	30 Days	60 Days	90 Days
Sales Funnel	Learn the funnel process, participate in sales meetings, and learn the prospects.	Take over in-bounds, funnel management, and forecasts.	Recommend a better sales management software to improve reporting. Assume full ownership.
Campaign Management	Learn the 2022 marketing calendar and align with sales campaigns.	Ensure that campaigns align with prospect targets and track coverage.	Produce and execute the sales campaign calendar.

Responsibility	30 Days	60 Days	90 Days
Sales Demo Support	Use every app by every vertical. Develop a demo path for each.	Be a resource for sales presentations.	Be able to conduct qualifying sales meetings independently.
Product Roadmaps	Read all the product marketing guides.	Understand the 2022 roadmap.	Produce sales and marketing materials for new roadmap items.
Prospect Qualification	Understand the list we use to qualify prospects.	Participate in qualifying prospects.	Independently qualify prospects.
Upsell Tracking	Learn our current clients and upsell opportunities.	Build an upsell tracker and report progress.	Own upsell support for account teams.
Sales Deck	Learn to present the standard deck and participate in meetings.	Independently present sales deck.	Own sales deck updates, optimization, and distribution.
Proposal Creation	Review existing proposals and pricing variables.	Participate in proposal and pricing development.	Own the ability to create a proposal.
Content Costs	Review content pricing structure.	Independently develop a content quote.	Be the master of content quoting for sales.
Deal Calculator	Learn the components of the deal calculator.	Be a resource for using the deal calculator.	Optimize the deal calculator.

Responsibility	30 Days	60 Days	90 Days
Product Documentation	Learn the library of key documents.	Become a resource for available docs.	Ownership in collaboration with product management.
Marxent License Agreement	Review and understand agreements.	Be able to prepare a draft agreement.	Independently prepare master agreements.
Sales Goals & KPIs	Understand strategic plan and role of sales.	Track goals.	Produce KPIs.
Team	Learn team structure.	Schedule meeting with functional leaders.	Have met all functional leaders.

Besides starting a job, another great time to create a ninety-day plan is when you're asking for a promotion. Every time an employee asks me for a promotion or a raise, I almost always say, "Build me a ninety-day plan for how you're going to accomplish your goals." Why? Because it tells me (if they complete it) they are serious about their request and taking on new responsibilities. An even better strategy is to not wait for your boss to make this ask. Show up with a ninety-day plan when you ask for your promotion or raise.

REMOTE WORK AND ... NINETY-DAY PLANS

Now more than ever, team members need to be more self-directed. Using ninety-day plans is paramount for new employees working remotely. We now require it for all new employees, regardless of role. If you were at a company when the pandemic started, it's hard to empathize with what it would be like to start a new job and try to become part of an established team and system once the pandemic was underway and everyone was working remotely. The ninety-day plan serves as a critical tool to make sure each new employee has a clear roadmap for what is expected of them. For the new employee, it's also comforting and reassuring to have a "map" they can follow as they learn a new organization. When COVID-19 hit, we updated our ninety-day-plan format to include a number of meetings to meet new team members. This formalized the process, gave new employees permission to set meetings, and accelerated their onboarding and company knowledge.

Building a Good Scope: The Foundation to Good Projects

No matter what project you may have ahead of you, you're going to need to build a shared framework to lay out your plan of attack. Or, in business parlance, a "scope." Whether you're developing a new product, drafting a statement of work for a new client, or creating a new training program, your personal process should include the fundamentals of building a good scope—a document that clearly communicates the shared goals, key activities, and the boundaries of a project.

A good scope is the foundation of any successful project. Interestingly, scope development isn't a discipline taught very often in college. The best scope education is provided by consulting firms like Ernst & Young, McKinsey, and Bain & Company. We often find that the best project scope writers come from the consulting firms that have formal training programs.

Employees who are good at scoping out a project are, in a word, *awesome*. In a second word, they're *invaluable*. They're usually very good problem solvers and become excellent critical thinkers. If you have the ability to build a good scope in your personal-process toolbox, you'll be highly valued, and it can take you far.

I've written thousands of scope documents in various forms, and I'm always on the hunt for the perfect framework to use to outline a project. This might be the most-often-used tool in my good habits toolbox. The following is my latest incarnation of my scoping framework:

1. **Project Vision:** A brief three-to-five-sentence summary of why a project is valuable to the company or client and the high-level desired outcomes.

2. **Measures of Success:** The metrics by which success will be measured (often called KPIs for key performance indicators), such as increase in average order value, reduction in product returns, or increased conversion rates. It's important to detail KPIs by stage of a project as

well. That is, what constitutes success in the first six months of a project versus the end of the first or second year.

3. **Key Stakeholders:** These are the people who you need to win over on a project. Another good practice is to identify both key stakeholders (the decision-makers) and potential detractors. Another good practice is to look for "hidden stakeholders" throughout the project. Trust me, they are there. These are the folks who, if you don't identify early in the project, can jump up and bite you. You'll want to update your scope document as additional stakeholders surface.

4. **Roles & Responsibilities:** This is a simple list of who is involved in the project and their respective contributions. Your goal here is (1) to avoid any conflicts or overlap, and (2) to denote people you need on the project whom you don't have yet.

5. **Project Requirements:** This is a concise summary of what features or capabilities need to be built. A big part of requirements is also identifying dependencies. That is, you can't do X if Y isn't done first.

6. **Major Deliverables:** This is a list of the major outcomes. That is, the benefits derived for the client, customer, or users.

7. **Major Milestones:** This is a list of progress points you'll need to hit during the project to know if you're on track to meet your final goals. Deliverables and milestones should be expressed in a Gantt chart.

8. **Major Assumptions:** Every project assumes some things to be true or not true. Your goal here is to make sure you have a good and shared understanding of what you're assuming to be the underlying truth.

9. **Constraints:** This is a list of what resources or limitations

you must work within. Common constraints include budget, time, and people available.

10. **Budget or Costs:** This is a summary of the financial resources you have available by category.

11. **Project Risks:** Risks are the most often neglected part of a project scope and the most dangerous. Taking the time to figure out where your big risks are allows you to make sure that you're focusing your energy on mitigating them early in the project (see "Tackle the Hard Things First and Ask for Help Early" on page 14).

I've found this scoping framework comes in handy in almost any situation where you have a team of people that needs to come together to solve a problem. I always have it close at hand as a quick framework to reference.

REMOTE WORK AND . . . PROJECT SCOPES

Creating a clear scope allows team members and key stakeholders to effectively organize around a project. Ambiguity will threaten the success of any project; ambiguity in a remote work situation will lead to certain failure. Galvanizing a team around a shared initiative or goal requires a clear set of roles, responsibilities, and expectations. Employees are often reticent to ask clarifying questions because they assume they're the only ones who may not be on the same page. This is much more likely in a remote work environment where the ability to read the room is much more difficult. Make sure to provide a safe forum for project participants to ask clarifying questions and to contribute to the scope. It's always a good practice to go around the room (whether on screen or IRL) and give everyone an opportunity to speak. Clear project scopes with clear responsibilities are now more important than ever.

How to Develop Good Judgment: The Heart of Leadership and Decision-Making

Jeff Bezos was asked what he looks for in employees and leaders, and his response wasn't the obvious things that might come to mind (e.g., smart, motivated, hardworking). Instead, he said that he looks for people who are right more often than not. "I want to see a track record of hard decisions that ended up being right. It's always better in business to be right than smart," Bezos shared. "Smart people can be wrong a lot." What he is talking about here is good judgment. After all, what could be more powerful than a team of people who all make consistently good decisions?

How does one develop good judgment? Is it something some folks are just born with? Or is good judgement something that must be learned or perhaps something that requires extensive experience? I'd submit that good judgment is something that you can have immediately and without a ton of practice. That is, if you have the right toolbox.

Being a boss is an interesting role. While there are fun parts of the job, most of your time you're actually helping fix problems and making difficult decisions.

Many managers, when faced with a sticky decision, will present a range of alternatives and perhaps their best recommendation. When I'm working with a manager on a decision that needs to be made and want to encourage development of their judgment, one of my favorite things to say is, "Managers present options; leaders make decisions," as a way of encouraging managers to make that next step into leadership.

Leadership in its simplest form is choosing between available options with existing information (which is often limited), then assuming responsibility for the outcome. Many team members don't make decisions because they don't want to assume responsibility for them. If you can make decisions and be willing to take responsibility for them, you'll stand out. In effect, you are "scaling" your boss, as that is one less decision she needs to make. So, it is important to understand that growth opportunities and leadership *require* you to make increasing decisions. With this as a backdrop, it makes sense that the logical next step in your path to management or leadership is to prepare yourself to make good decisions.

What does good decision-making look like? Well, unfortunately there aren't any obviously "good decisions" while you're making them. You only know it was a bad decision when it turns out bad. It follows then that the practice of good decision making is really a practice of "finding the truest option" by eliminating the options that are "least true." Think of it like using the scientific method where your goal is not to find "proof" but rather disproving all the other alternatives. So, our job is to eliminate the bad options and then have the courage to move forward with the most probable option. The good news is that nobody expects you to be right all the time. But what does it take to develop a "track record" of good decisions that would impress Mr. Bezos? Misjudgment, it turns out, is largely the problem, according to behavioral psychology.

There is a large body of research in behavioral psychology on why we make bad decisions, but for my money, the most accessible resource comes from Charlie Munger, the famed investor (and longtime partner of Warren Buffett) in his noted speech "The Psychology of Human Misjudgment." Charlie, in a nutshell, asserts that we're usually our own problem. That is, our fears, biases, and ego. "When I saw this patterned irrationality, which was so extreme, and I had no theory or anything to deal with it, but I could see that it was extreme, and I could see that it was patterned, I just started to create my own system of psychology, partly by casual reading, but largely from personal experience, and I used that pattern to help me get through life," Charlie shared in a speech at Harvard in 1995. See, even famed investors and billionaires need a good habits toolbox.

There is a great YouTube video where you can watch an animated video of Charlie's speech.* I often use this video in leadership development training. It's simple, funny, and very

_____

* "Billionaire Charlie Munger—The Psychology of Human Misjudgment," January 17, 2018, video, 14:41, https://www.youtube.com/watch?v=TUA7PS5-y5o.

easy to understand.

Here is the simplified "Charlie Checklist" I reference when I have an important decision to make sure I'm as objective as I can be about the decision. While there are several more in Charlie's list, I've found these five are the most powerful:

1.   Am I choosing a direction because the alternative is unthinkable? Am I in denial?

This one is tough. Most people who are in denial can't self-diagnose. Think of a parent who finds out their lovely teen—who they believe can do no wrong—is accused of being a bully at school. While it's obvious to the rest of the world that Jimmy needs an attitude adjustment, think of the fevered passion that a parent exhibits to defend his or her child—perhaps even going to incredible extremes in defense of their little tyrant. That's denial. Think of the alcoholic or other addict who will rationalize their way through decades of addiction, failing to admit they have a problem and need help. That's denial. Denial is almost always an emotionally charged situation that lives at the root of your ego or greatest fears. If you're in denial, your chances of getting through it alone are low.

In the workplace, denial may crop up in any number of circumstances. A product may not be getting market acceptance, a competitor's product may be better than yours, your customers may not be happy, or that whiz-bang high-flying exec you told everybody would turn around a department is a total dud. I've made bad calls on all of the above.

Overcoming denial most often requires that you swallow your ego or face your fears. And after you finally come to terms with the right thing to do, there is usually a bunch of work that follows to fix the problem. Having good people around you or a mentor who can help you through denial is paramount, especially as you take on increasing levels of responsibility. I've had several mentors fill this role for me over the years, but I've committed to keeping one at my side at all times. Ed Woiteshek, my most active board member at Marxent, is my current "denial coach." My "favorite" sessions are meeting with him to work through a bit of denial, even when I didn't know the topic was on the agenda. It's tough medicine to swallow, but I always come out of our discussions clear minded and ready to take on the issue.

2. **Am I trusting an "expert's" advice even though my own observations draw me to a different conclusion? Am I suffering from what Stanley Milgram coined as "agency theory?" That is, relying too heavily on another person who is supposed to have specific domain expertise.**

I'm not fond of lawyers. Not because they charge too much, but because they are highly trained in persuasion. They are masters of "agency." Political and religious leaders are also excellent with agency. It's incredibly powerful, and can, when in the wrong hands, be insidious. Charlie uses the following example in his Harvard speech that is a real gut punch and perhaps the most extreme example of the power of agency.

Stanley Milgram is the famous behavioral psychologist who conducted mock shock experiments using a fake expert (a doctor) to see if he could get participants to execute orders that were obviously cruel and hurtful. Milgram recruited students to flip a series of switches on a panel that represented increasing levels of electric shock. The recipient of the shock treatment was an actor hidden in another room that the subject of the experiment could hear but couldn't see. The "expert" doctor—white lab coat and all—would ask the participant to flip a switch, after which an audible "yelp" would come from the other room. Then the doctor would ask the subject to flip yet another and another switch that would "increase" the level of the electric shock until the actor in the other room was screaming bloody murder. Each time the participant would hesitate or show concern, the highly credible "doctor" would calmly and confidently confirm that this was a valid experiment and that he had the credentials and authority to conduct it.

Milgram, whose family was subjected to Nazi atrocities, pursued his research in a mission to understand why "good" people could find themselves part of an assembly line of mass murder.

The result of Milgram's experiment? A whopping 65 percent of participants flipped every cruel switch. *Flip zap, flip zap, flip ZAP, flip ZAP, flip ZAP!* Sixty-five percent blindly followed the direction of an "expert." Behavior so irrational, as Charlie would say, that it questions if we're all walking through life blindly bending to the wills of those around us.

Lawyers are often fond of using the phrase, "These are standard terms." What they are really saying is, "For those of us educated and experienced in the profession, we have agreed that this is reasonable. If you don't agree, you're demonstrating your ignorance and inexperience. Trust me." While "these are standard terms" seems totally innocuous, it has a seedy underbelly. Venture capitalists are also really good with the "standard terms" line. Watch out for this one in particular.

Avoiding the agency effect is difficult. Particularly when you're actively seeking advice from others to help make a decision. This is a circumstance where you need to listen to your heart and have the courage to ask enough questions to surface all the facts.

3. **Am I choosing a direction because it is a position I held previously, regardless of new information? Is my ego getting in the way of hearing new information?**

Unlike the first two on this list, the third item on the Charlie judgment checklist only requires an open mind to master. Ah, if it were only that easy to have an open mind. Behavioral psychologists call this behavior "confirmation bias," which in layman's terms simply means we all like our own ideas. The bifurcation of the news media by political ideologies is a good example of confirmation bias. We all gorge on our already closely held beliefs daily, almost without thought. The advertising algorithms from our favorite social media platforms are like crack for confirmation bias junkies, shooting us up minute by minute, day after day. We might tell ourselves we're above this sort of belief system but be careful casting stones. We're all susceptible.

Let's imagine you're preparing a presentation for your sales team that asserts that selling into a particular vertical will yield the greatest results. You believe this to be true based on your own experience. And it may well be. But you're a sample set of one, and there is surely not enough information upon which to draw a confident conclusion. But you've already shared your view publicly. Now you feel your reputation is at stake. As you prepare your presentation, how likely is it that you're going to report, let alone search for, information that is counter to your original position?

Overcoming confirmation bias requires three traits: (1) a

high degree of self-awareness, (2) a desire to get at the truth over being "right," and (3) enough humility to change your mind when the data points you in a different direction. Yeah, it ain't easy. But if you can master your own biases, you'll be a much better decision-maker for it—and really, probably a much more open-minded human being too.

4. **Am I making a given decision because I think it meets the expectations of others? Am I trying to make everyone happy? Am I fearful that I'll be kicked out of the group for a contrary view? This phenonium is commonly referred to as "groupthink."**

Humans are herd animals. We seek protection in groups. While we no longer need our tribe to help us fight off sabre-tooth tigers, our need to belong to something and to feel protected by a tribe is still there deeply imbedded in our lower brains. I read an article once that said we develop our speaking accent from our peer groups versus immediate families and that our speech patterns will change almost seamlessly to signal that we're a member of whatever group we need to belong to at any given time.

I have a funny personal story related to this. I had never been a part of large corporation before we sold our little twenty-person startup to NCR—a global software company. But suddenly I was thrust into a hundred-plus-year-old, six-thousand-person company. I was definitely a fish out of water. Over the next three years, I scooped up the language of big corporations and quickly made it my own. It was almost frightening how effortlessly I did this. I became the master of corporate jargon, offering to "ping" people back when I need to follow up. I was "circling back around, sticking things in my wheelhouse, touching base, leveling up, assessing bandwidth, and moving needles." We'll have some more fun with jargon in a bit, but keep this in mind for now: if the need to belong can modify our vocabulary so easily, imagine the impact it can have on our decision-making where the stakes are even higher.

Groupthink is very real. It's the easiest way to fit in and be safe. Not only has groupthink sunk many once storied businesses, but it also quite literally sunk the *Titanic*. So how do you overcome groupthink? First, hopefully you are part of an organization that values diverse opinions.

I've found that the best way to make sure groupthink isn't driving decisions is to, ironically, make the surfacing of alternative viewpoints a group activity. Here's how this works. Once you've found that your group or team is close to reaching consensus on a topic, you build a safe environment for members of the team who may not agree to voice their view. You might say for instance, "Okay team, it looks like we're largely aligned here. Let's all take some time to brainstorm why this might not be the best course of action." Now everyone is free to test the decision without fear of being kicked out of the group. What I've found is that the discussion then gets very fluid. Ideas flow back and forth easily. And often a better course of action emerges that has shared ownership.

5. **Am I making a decision because the investment or effort has already been expended and we "want to see something come of it?" Do I have the courage to change course even though it will be painful and time consuming?**

Here's an oldie but goodie: the sunk-investment challenge.

A decision at one point in time may have been the perfect decision, but the world can quickly change around us. What do you do in these circumstances even after the money has been spent, and it is now clear that what was once perhaps a good decision now needs to be reevaluated?

In the first company we founded in 1999, we built a nifty advertising platform that would allow us to distribute different promotions to different audiences based on a given consumer purchase behavior. Shoppers at a local Safeway or Meijer grocery stores could scan their loyalty card and receive a promotion for an item that would likely be of interest. If you're buying a lot of diapers, you'll likely be interested in baby formula. If you're eating a lot of salty snacks, you'll likely be interested in a cold Coke or Pepsi to wash it down.

As part of this solution, we had also developed a small seven-inch touch screen computer equipped with a barcode scanner and a wireless card. So now not only could we provide these targeted advertisements at the checkout (yes, those long receipts . . . you're welcome), but shoppers could scan their loyalty cards in-aisle and check for offers. While these kinds of solutions are commonplace today, this was revolutionary in 2000. Single-board computers that didn't require fans and camera-based barcode scanners allowed you to build a small computer about the size of an iPad that could be mounted anywhere in a retail store that had power available.

We had spent thousands of dollars building this first-generation hardware, and we had set up manufacturers; we had our first clients operational, and we were ready to take over retail. While we had heard that others (IBM, NCR, Fujitsu, etc.) were also developing devices, we were certain that we were first to market and that we had the right solution (see confirmation bias). Full steam ahead. We continued to invest for more than a year, and we were now ready to show off our wares at the biggest retail event in the world: the National Retail Federation Show in New York.

New York in January is the worst. Our hotel was eight or so blocks from the Javits Center. It was setup day, and the doors would open the next morning. Every major tech decision-maker in retail would be walking by our booth. We boxed up our hardware and skated to the Javits Center in our dress shoes. Heads held high and full of hope, we crossed the threshold into the conference center and then . . . nearly fainted. While the year before we had the only such device on the floor, this year the tradeshow floor gleamed and glistened with shiny touchscreen devices with scanners and wireless cards. No less than fifty companies were hawking similar tech. And all of them were larger than us by orders of magnitude.

It was clear in an instant that we should have exited the hardware game a year ago and focused on our software solution, but we had made the investment and couldn't bear the thought of abandoning what we thought was a good decision, even though all the data was there in front of us to make that decision. Team members had voiced their concerns, but we didn't listen. Thank goodness we were able to course-correct and put all of our focus on our software product, but it was a decision that nearly bankrupted the company at the time.

Making a bad decision because you feel "pot committed" in a given direction is easy to do. We were a fast-moving, scrappy startup. Imagine course-correcting in a massive company after billions of dollars have been spent and thousands of people have been mobilized. Few have done it successfully. Xerox, Kodak, Circuit City, Blockbuster, Blackberry, Yahoo,

JCPenney, Sears, RadioShack, Borders, Palm, Toys "R" Us, and AOL all have harrowing stories to tell, I imagine.

REMOTE WORK AND . . . GOOD JUDGMENT

Learning how someone thinks and how he or she reaches decisions takes time. It requires working together on multiple projects, hundreds of big and small interactions, experience with how someone responds to adversity, and experience with how someone interacts with others. Remote work dramatically reduces the number of chances you get to learn this about someone, and it increases the time it takes to get a feel for how confident you are in others. The good judgment framework can be a powerful tool to demonstrate to your boss or coworkers how you process information and come to a decision. Being able to communicate that you've used a decision-making framework like Charlie's Checklist gives you a chance to "show your work" and build confidence in your judgment. For instance, you might say on the topic of confirmation bias something like, "Our original recommendation was to expand our services to Europe first. After a detailed analysis, our recommendation has remained unchanged. In our analysis, we did invest heavily in researching alternative options, and we consulted experts with opposing views." This approach demonstrates that you have a decision-making framework, and you were careful not to fall prey to confirmation bias.

The Secret to (Most) Decision-Making

Assuming responsibility for making decisions may seem daunting, especially in light of the cautionary tales of Blockbuster and its many peers (RIP). But most of us aren't involved in these kinds of major strategic decisions. Most decisions we make are on a lot smaller scale. There is, however, a little secret that once you understand, makes making the decision to make decisions a whole lot easier.

Ready?

Most decisions are never final. They are more like adjusting your steering wheel in your car by a few degrees and then finding you need to adjust again, and again, and again. There are, of course, major strategic decisions that get made in an organization that can make or break a company. But for the vast majority of managers and leaders, decisions are simply fact-finding missions to find out if you're pursuing the correct path. If you find you're wrong, you simply adjust course and move on.

I have a simple question I ask that was taught to me by my mentor, Ed Woiteshek. When you need to make a decision, first simply ask yourself, *Is this decision reversible?* If the decision *isn't* reversible, you'll need to spend a good amount of time really evaluating your options. However, if a decision *is* reversible, the amount of time you need to validate the decision goes way down. In these cases, make the best decision, learn quickly, and adjust. By using this methodology, you'll end up reaching a solution much faster.

In practice, this is the first question I ask team members when they're struggling with a decision. In 90 percent of the cases, the decision is reversible. So, then you can quickly move to the best recommendation based on the information you have at hand and keep moving.

As we've examined, making decisions is fundamental to leadership. The other major responsibility of leaders is to create other leaders. I read a great meme once that said, "You're not a leader until you've created another leader and that leader is capable of creating another leader." I loved this quote. At its core, it is saying that to be a leader you need to develop good judgment and then show others how to develop good judgment. Charlie's Checklist is the perfect tool for this job.

Building Confidence: Finding the Fastest, Smallest Unit of Success

Everyone is looking for assurance that they are on the right path. When we're on a road trip with family, even with Google Maps, it's always comforting to see a road sign that says your destination is ahead of you. The same logic applies for most business projects. Your boss or leadership is looking for the "smallest and fastest unit of success" to build confidence that your project is headed in the right direction.

In 2017, we were implementing the first rollout of virtual reality (VR) room design in retail with Macy's. This was cutting-edge tech at the time, and nobody had any real empirical evidence that store associates or customers would adopt the solution. There was a question at the beginning of the project about the number of stores we wanted to install for the pilot. Now, imagine you're the CEO of Macy's for a moment. Let's say the definition of success was driving a million dollars per month per store in VR sales. You have the option to install twenty stores or ten stores or even one store. What do you do?

Before you answer, here is how CEOs think: They take the best result they can get out of a single store to understand the potential of a project, then they multiply it by their total number of stores. Then they'll discount that number assuming some operational inefficiencies. So, given this, if you have only a limited number of resources for installation, training, support, and so on, would you spread your resources over twenty locations or over one location?

We partnered with Macy's and ultimately decided on three stores with the goal of making at least one of them wildly successful. We picked three instead of one just in case there was something about a single store (e.g., poor manager support, a bad internet connection, uninspired associates) that prevented us from getting the desired result. Concentrating your resources on the smallest unit of success helps win over naysayers, secure additional resources, build confidence amongst the team, and develop a template of success to copy at a larger scale.

REMOTE WORK AND . . . THE SMALLEST UNIT OF SUCCESS

We all feel less connected in the remote world. Think of all the projects pre-COVID-19, when you were able to be on-site with a team, customer, or end-users to evaluate the effectiveness of an implementation. You could witness firsthand how a project was going. While we can still collect analytics and draw some conclusions, it's very difficult to collect and assess anecdotal evidence or read body language that is often critical to gaining key insights. The effort that is required to collect customer or user feedback is now much higher, so spending energy and resources to ensure you can move forward becomes even more important. Of course, the fundamentals of finding the fastest and smallest unit of success still require that you use other good work habits such as employing a good scoping framework and applying good judgment by using tools like the Charlie Checklist.

Grit: The Great Separator

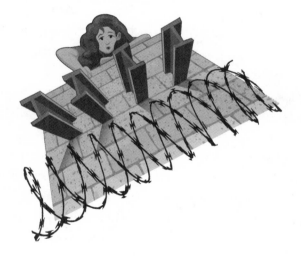

Angela Duckworth is a professor of psychology at the University of Pennsylvania. She shared a very popular TED Talk in April 2013 based on her research into why people succeed called "Grit: The Power of Passion and Perseverance." Duckworth concluded that grit is the great separator—the reason people really succeed. Not privilege, opportunity, intelligence, nor creativity. Good old grit. My experience working with hundreds of employees has yielded the same undeniable conclusion. Grit wins every single time. Every time.

But what is grit and where does one get it? Well, simply stated, grit is the belief that there is *always* a way forward. And if not forward, then over, around, under, between, across, or if necessary, straight though. The best employees believe this. And bosses love grit. Grit is the mental fortitude to persevere toward a long-term goal and to find creative solutions when they aren't immediately evident.

But where does the "grit gene" come from? Why do some have it and others not so much? Duckworth's research suggests grit may come from passion, curiosity, practice, ego, purpose, personal pride, insecurity, or a positive self-image. That's a short way of saying, grit could come from any number of places or combinations thereof.

Here's what I do know: I've never been able to teach grit. This is one of the items in your toolbox that you'll need to build for yourself if you don't have it. But I do have an idea of where it comes from that might help you on your quest.

I believe grit most often comes from early life experiences where you've experienced the pleasure of completing a task or winning championship or solving a puzzle and then having someone you love or respect tell you they're proud of you and your efforts. That positive reinforcement is such a powerful high that we then spend the rest of our lives trying to replicate it. Those early experiences become your identity and place in the world, and once you have a place in world, you'll do almost anything to hold onto it. Accordingly, I think that our number one job as parents is to help our children find their identity, because once they have it, they'll avoid bad decisions that put their identity at risk. No identity, no direction, nothing to lose, no perseverance, no grit. I believe it's that simple.

In job interviews, I dig for that moment where a candidate's grit "turned on." Where and when did they develop their identity and their passion. It's usually not hard to find. Sometimes it's from a positive experience. Sometimes it's from a negative experience. I don't think it really matters why as long as it's there *now*.

When I was seven or eight, I was working at my father's sporting goods store helping with inventory, sweeping floors, and folding t-shirts. I was doodling on a piece of paper siting at his desk in the office. I drew a picture of a character with a basketball for a head, a football for a torso, a hockey stick and bat for legs, and rackets for arms. I put a big logo on the top that spelled out "Sportsman—Your all sports enthusiast" in bright red and yellow letters. My dad came in and said, "Wow, that's really cool. We should put that on one of our t-shirts and copyright it."

And . . . BOOM!

It was like a bolt of lightning hit me in the center of my brain. I knew who I was at that very moment and work every day to recreate the joy I felt. I was going into business! Now all I needed to do was to figure out what a copyright was.

From these early moments you repeat "grit behavior." Focusing and finishing becomes a habit. An obsession with seeing something through reinforces identity. Of course, life is life, and you won't be successful every single time. But in order to have the grit to win most of the time, you must know what "finishing" feels like. Unfortunately, giving up is also a pattern of behavior that repeats and repeats.

If you know you don't have grit, it's not too late. Decide who you are, take a step, even a small one, and finish. Share your journey with someone you love or respect and watch the "grit light" switch on.

REMOTE WORK AND . . . GRIT

Perseverance and self-reliance have become even more important with remote work, especially if you're new to an organization. We've learned firsthand that new employees lacking the grit gene struggle to find their footing. Many of the tools, documents, processes, and systems that a new employee may need to do their job are learned by watching and learning from existing employees. Having someone sitting next to you to do job shadowing has always been an effective way to learn. Now that we're remote, companies need to make major investments in remote training, knowledge bases, and other tools to help employees be successful. But that's still not enough in many cases. A remote employee must be resourceful themselves and be proactive in their own development and onboarding. Employees with the grit gene are much more likely to dig in and find what they need to be successful.

Creating Structure in White Space: Don't Let Uncertainty Slow You Down

It's obvious that setting goals is critical to measuring growth, progress, and efficiency. If you're involved in a long-standing project or you have last year's sales numbers to reference, goal setting is relatively easy. But how do you set goals in scenarios where you don't have any prior data to reference? What if the variables that go into calculating a good return on investment aren't immediately obvious?

There are many scenarios at work where you don't know enough to create an objective, and you're working in totally new white space. Or, I should say, you don't know enough *yet*. There is an old expression in business that goes, "What doesn't get measured, doesn't get managed." Which is another way of saying, "How can you improve if you didn't keep track of what was previously accomplished?"

While working on the Macy's virtual reality project, one key component of program success was going to be sales associate adoption. However, colleague adoption was one of many variables; others were increase in average order value, reduction in returns, number of consumers that would take advantage of the tech, overall store traffic, and so on. There were many ways to hit break-even on the program and then ultimately a good return on investment. But this was the first implementation of VR in retail history, so we had little to go off of. Total white space.

So, then what does one do in this scenario? Well, you make something up, learn, and refine. You create structure and metrics and then you simply improve. You take some combination of the "input" variables, take an educated guess, communicate the key metrics with *unjustified* confidence, and you move forward. Too often employees "freeze" in these kinds of situations—they're afraid to make a mistake or look silly. Hot tip: We already know you're making it up. Hell, *we're* making it up. What we're looking for is the willingness to build a framework, move forward, learn, and adjust.

In the Macy's VR project, we didn't have store traffic, so right away we were missing a big input. We just estimated that 10 percent of consumers would take advantage of the system. Then we said store associate usage should be measured in frequency of use, and we defined an "active" user as more than three times per month. And then we said we would grow from 30 percent of associates being active in the first three months, and then 40 percent in the subsequent three months, and so on. Then we said the average order value would increase by 50 percent, and we said returns would go down by 20 percent.

All of this was *100 percent completely made up*. A complete swag.

Then we just started. Installs, training, integrations, etc. As the data came in, we were way off in some areas and not too far off in others. But it didn't matter. What mattered is that we had a shared understanding of what we were looking for. After six months, we simply looked at the data, adjusted the goals, and moved forward.

Bosses love employees who can create structure even if there are many unknowns. Because creating structure creates focus and concentration of energy on the right variables. Then, results emerge and you simply adjust. What's important is that uncertainty doesn't keep you from moving forward because moving forward is the only way to learn.

A Final Word on Good Personal-Process Habits

We've explored a number of techniques for building good personal-process habits. I chose to share these personal-process habits in large part because these are among the most common topics where team members have needed support. While good additions to your personal-process toolbox, there is no doubt that you'll build your own toolbox over the course of your career. I'd encourage you to keep track of them and keep them close at hand. And more importantly, take the time to share them with others who need help on their personal-process journey.

CHAPTER 2
GOOD COMMUNICATION HABITS

REMEMBERING FACTS IS OFTEN difficult. But we all remember, almost effortlessly, the words to songs we haven't heard in years. Likewise, stories and how they made us feel when we heard them stay with us long after the details are forgotten. As Maya Angelou, the famous poet and civil rights leader, said, "I've learned that people will forget what you said, people will forget what you did, but people will never forget how you made them feel."

Stories are an incredibly effective way to communicate, to learn important lessons for your toolbox, and to mentor others.

One of my favorite books is *Into the Wild*—a story based on the real life of Christopher McCandless. After graduating from college, McCandless abandoned society for total freedom and solitude. For me, the story is about freeing oneself from control systems and societal expectations with the goal of finding true happiness.

Nearly everyone has had this fantasy of being free from the opinions, expectations, and dependencies of others. For most, the notion of escaping the grind of competing priorities, ambiguity, bureaucracy, and unrealistic expectations is tempting. In the story, McCandless abandons family, money, and opportunity for a life alone in the wilderness, but, in a final moment of irony, he has the deathbed revelation that, "Happiness is only real when shared."

During my first real job, I learned a lesson about this from my boss and mentor, Chuck Wise. I was working at the Office of Advancement while in grad school at Purdue University and was charged with leading a team on a major project. Toward the end of the project, Chuck requested a comprehensive update on each team's area of responsibility. A week following his request, I presented a twenty-page report for his review. A few days later, Chuck gave it back to me with one recurring edit—every "I" and "me" in the report was circled in red. After scratching my head for a bit, the message was clear. Every "I" was a statement that *my* contributions were somehow above the work of the team. I had made this happen. I willed our results into existence. I made all the right decisions. I kept us on budget. And in summary, I deserved all the credit. He had presented me with a golden opportunity to elevate the contributions of everyone on the team, and I had failed to recognize them. *I* was an idiot.

Chuck called me into his office the next day. He smiled and took the report from my hand, crossed out the first "I" in the report and wrote "We." Then he patted me on the back and said, "No one does it alone, son." He was right. It had been a tremendous team effort.

We revisited and rewrote the report from the "we" perspective. This small shift in tone and perspective changed the entire tenor of the report. More importantly, it reinforced the collective ownership of our success and the team's motivation to charge the next hill.

"We-speak" may feel like a control system that swallows individuals into a collective, but the "we worldview" actually does the opposite. When a manager hears an employee bragging on the contributions of others and the team, he or she can't help but think, *Wow, this person can lead. He or she knows how to bring the best out in others. Definite management potential.*

Both Chuck and McCandless were right. Like happiness, success is only real when shared.

This chapter is dedicated to good communication habits like "communicating in we."

Don't Hide Bad News: Balanced Communication and the Value of Bad News

As a leader, I love bad news. Well, what I should say is that I hate 100 percent good news. Why? Because in life and work there is *always* bad news. You lose deals, projects are late, shipments don't come in on time, good employees leave, software has bugs. This is work in real life. The question from a CEO or any boss's eyes is whether they *know* about it so they can help solve the problem before it's too late.

Your boss isn't stupid (I hope). He or she also knows the world isn't perfect. What a boss wants is *balanced* communication. "Here are the positives. Here are the negatives." If you choose to only communicate the positives or consistently paint a rosy picture, you're not making yourself look good. You're actually doing the opposite—you're hurting your credibility. Even if in that rare instance there is no bad news to report, communicate that you've thought about it by simply saying,

"No bad news to report at this time." I like to say to employees, "Always shoot for at least 20 percent bad news." Here is an example sent to Gail (the boss):

> *Hi, Gail.*
>
> *We've heard that we're in the pole position on the Wilson deal. We have a strong champion in Bill Sommers, and he's helping us navigate the final few approvals and executive presentations.*
>
> *While we feel good about our odds, the team is thinking through what can go wrong. We have a stakeholder at Wilson who is loyal to the incumbent vendor. This guy Tom continues to challenge our financial assumptions . . .*

Why would Gail, "the boss," like this communication? Because she can help you solve problems. She doesn't need to help when things are good. Gail, if she is a good leader, is hardwired to look for where she can pitch in to address conflicts, find resources, overcome roadblocks, or call in a favor. That's not to say that a good boss won't get a little prickly when hearing bad news. That's normal. But a good boss will process it quickly, slow his or her heart rate, and start to help you find answers.

Bottom line: It's hard to believe good news when there is no counterpoint. It comes down to a case of credibility. And while it may be hard to admit that something isn't going as expected, bad news can have a positive effect when shared early and clearly. The prompt sharing of bad news can keep small issues small, guide the setting of expectations, and help build trust among team members.

REMOTE WORK AND ... BAD NEWS

The importance of balanced communications and sharing bad news early has been intensified in a post-pandemic world. We've learned that the ability of team members to feel comfortable with and confident in sharing bad news, not surprisingly, is directly related to how the recipient of the bad news responds. If the receiver blows up or is quick to assign blame, the odds that a team member is going to be apt to share bad news a second time obviously goes down.

Moreover, the default assumption for most employees in organizations is that bad news will be met with disappointment and anger. I had a boss myself whose face would turn so red that you'd swear his hair was going to catch on fire. I've also been that boss on more than one occasion. If you're a new remote employee who has never even met your boss in person, your default assumption is likely going to be that bad news will be met with ire. It is now even more important that companies develop a system for the safe sharing of bad news, encouraging it regularly, and making it part of the company culture.

One technique I learned from Josh Linkner, a *New York Times* bestselling author on creativity in the workplace, is to make the sharing of bad news a part of company meetings. He calls this technique "F-Up Fridays." His suggestion is to make time on all team calls for team members to share their foibles as a way of communicating that bad news is an important part of your culture. We took Josh's advice and dedicated one of our all-team meetings recently to sharing our f-ups. It was a blast. We encouraged company leaders to start as a way to grease the wheels a bit and employees jumped right in. It was like a giant therapy session. It was also a lot of fun. I think most employees found it incredibly liberating.

Jargon Doesn't Move the Needle, and Stop Pinging Everyone

We talked about the phenomenon of jargon in the workplace in chapter 1 as a way to assimilate and belong. But jargon can also be damaging to your personal communication habits. Let's look at some common examples we all hear and have likely used. When we hold "empower hours" with employees on good work habits, this is one of the most fun sessions. I like to ask participants to raise their hands if they've used one of the following phrases. Feel free to play along.

*"I'm going to **circle back** around with you . . ."*—Are we on a Disney carousel?

*"I'll schedule time for us to **touch base** each week."*—We're playing baseball?

*"I just wanted to **reach out** and see if we can be of service."*—The Four Tops put this to a great melody.

*"We're going to take this to the **next level**."*—Which level are we at now? How many levels are there?

*"This is going to be a **next generation** solution."*—I blame Star Trek for this one. Make it so, Lieutenant Commander La Forge.

*"We need to **level up** our thinking."*—Mario Bros. anyone? I thought we were already going next level.

*"Guys we're not going to have the **bandwidth** to get this done."*—We're only at two bars, folks.

*"Why would we do this if it isn't going to **move the needle** for us?"*—Vroom, vroom.

*"Look, at the **end of the day**, we need a solution that works for everyone."*—What is the official date for this one anyway? And will there be a happy hour when it's done?

*"This is right in our **wheelhouse** . . ."*—Oh, you're handling the Smith account and captaining a ship? Impressive.

*"We're just **few clicks short** of where we want to be."*—I think this is another nautical term we're going to execute from our wheelhouse.

*Any sentence with the word **"ping"** in it.*—We've graduated from our boat to a submarine.

*"We're going to have to schedule a **deep dive** next week to figure this out."*—Well, we're prepared for this now that we're in a sub.

"Business speak" in the workplace is fascinating. We add a few and subtract a few each year, but the practice persists, nonetheless.

While jargon is kind of fun, it is a form of pseudo-intellectualism. It's filler language for those who didn't want to invest the time to respond thoughtfully. It can also be a form of evasion or an attempt to demonstrate participation without preparation. And it's terribly unoriginal.

Speak plainly and clearly with a desire to help the recipient to receive the communication effectively—not to impress and obfuscate. If nothing else, be novel. You're much more likely to be heard than in the echo chamber that is business jargon.

Carving Pumpkins and Naming Your Story

We've all been in meetings or attended presentations where we can barely stay awake and the odds of retaining any information is low. Of course, we all think our own presentations are riveting. But why is it that good presentations really stand out? What is the presenter doing differently that we can use to actually make our own presentation stellar?

Dan Gilbert is the founder of Quicken Loans, one of the largest mortgage lenders in the United States. Dan is a major investor in Marxent, the company we run now, which gave us access to hear Dan present on multiple occasions. And boy, *he is riveting*. Absolutely enthralling. You can't look away, and you find yourself hanging on every word. What's interesting is that he's not a very good speaker if you were to judge him by the typical criteria. He's not particularly eloquent. He's not traditionally charismatic. He often struggles to even find the right word to express his thought. He is definitely not polished;

he often starts and stops and goes off topic. He doesn't even use visual aids most of the time. So, what makes him so good? He is the master of framing up a topic in such a way as to keep you mentally and emotionally engaged. And he uses a not-so-obvious technique that will be a great addition to your communication toolbox.

A few years back we went to Detroit for a leadership event along with the leaders of several other startups. About two hundred folks were in attendance. Dan was introduced, then he fumbled with his mic a bit.

He finally spoke. "Anybody here ever carve a pumpkin?"

What?! Pumpkins? Where the heck is this going?

He continued . . .

"I was out with my family this weekend, and we went to a pumpkin patch. My whole life we've been carving pumpkins by cutting a hole in the top and then scooping out the guts with a spoon out of this little hole. And then when you put a candle in, you have to light it and then try and place it in the bottom of the pumpkin without burning your hand. But this weekend I saw a kid carving a pumpkin from the bottom. He sliced off the bottom a few inches from the base, easily pulled out the innards, then simply placed a lit candle in the bottom of the base of the pumpkin and placed the top of the pumpkin on the base. Freaking genius. Why doesn't everybody do it this way? It's so much easier! Why is it that this kid was doing it like this? What made him think so differently? Opportunities in business and in your companies are all around you. *How do you unlock the creativity in your teams to find new ways of working?*"

Dan used a simple story we could all relate to, then he ended with a clear and direct question that made your brain want to pay attention to the rest of his talk until you knew the answer.

Just brilliant. Before trying to convey his observations on creative problem solving, he created a hole in my head (much like the pumpkin) that now needed to be filled with the answer. This is what all great presenters do. Before they convey information, they build a place in your head for it to live.

Whether you're addressing team members in a meeting, presenting to your boss, or having a quarterly business review with a customer, this framework is always effective. The most important part of any presentation is framing up why everyone is here. Once the "why" is set, everyone now has a mental map for where the conversation is going and can stay actively engaged. You're setting an expectation about the topic, desired outcomes, and how others can contribute all in a single statement. This technique also makes you much easier to listen to. I call this communication framework "naming your story."

What does "naming your story" mean? Every time you call a meeting, get in front of a client or make a presentation, you are telling a story. All stories have a beginning, middle, and end. If you start to think of your interactions in this way, you'll realize that it makes sense to structure your thoughts and name your story so that everyone in the room can track what you're talking about. Not only does this keep you from losing track of your storyline by getting lost in the details, but it ensures that you'll clearly communicate whatever it is you've set out to get across.

Let's look at an example of a bad and then a good version of the same opening of a meeting. Imagine you, me, and five other team members have been called to a meeting organized by Nicole, an account manager. And Nicole says the following:

Good morning, everyone. Brad Billings, you all know Brad, right? Brad is our main point of contact at Thompson. Well, he is not happy. We had a call late yesterday and broke the news that we're going to miss the deadline. This is after we told him we were going to hit the deadline just a few weeks ago. I don't know if there is anything we can do at this point, but I figured I'd get us all in the same room to see if anyone has any ideas . . .

Yuck, you're probably thinking. You've probably been in a meeting that has opened like this. It's easy to fall into this trap, this communication style. Not only is it unstructured, but it's also frustrating for the listener, and it doesn't build confidence. Let's try the same meeting again, but this time Nicole is going to name her story.

Good morning, everyone. Thank you for your time. **Today we're talking about how we're going to address our risk of missing our deadline on the Thompson project (the name of your story).** *We have three known options to consider, as well as any others that surface from the discussion today. We need to come out of this meeting with our recommendation, action items, and owners, and we need to communicate our plan to the client by the end of the day today. Any questions? Ok, let's start with the facts . . .*

This approach frames the discussion and sets expectations. Everyone in the meeting now has a "mental map" for how to contribute and a definition of outcomes. No matter the venue, taking the time to name your story is a powerful way to improve the productivity of your communications.

Holding the attention of an audience in a live meeting is challenging. Holding the attention of an audience in a post-pandemic world is next to impossible. Kids, animals, email, and Slack are all easy distractions. I once had a Zoom call with a guy who was literally preparing his breakfast and then started eating and talking with his mouth half full. Geez, bro. It's just way too easy for all of us to multitask now. I'm a big believer in "camera's on" during Zoom meetings. I ask it of employees in all internal meetings. While this helps, it's ultimately up to the presenter to make sure he or she is framing up the conversation to keep folks engaged. Clearly communicating the purpose and goal of any meeting is now more important than ever. Making sure to ask questions that drive participation and engagement is critical.

Respond to Requests like a Pro

Chuck sent me an email and asked if I would take on evaluating a potential scanning vendor. It was 1999, and we were looking for a solution that could turn paper donor records into digital assets that could be indexed and searched more easily. His email went something like, "Can you take the lead on researching and recommending three to four vendors that we can bring in for further evaluation?" I had hoped I'd get that opportunity, and I quickly responded with, "Got it." My response was promptly followed by a lunch invite. And I was like, "Oh man, what did I do this time?" So, I steeled myself for another mentoring session.

We sat down for lunch, exchanged a few pleasantries, and then Chuck asked me, "You *got* what?"

"I was just confirming that I'd take on your request to evaluate scanning vendors," I stammered.

"I understand, but what does *got* mean?" Chuck replied.

"Well, I imagine that it will probably take a week to research top firms in the space," I said.

"And then what?" he asked.

"Well, then I'll probably build a structure that we can use to evaluate the strengths and weaknesses of each vendor," I responded.

"And then what?" he continued.

"Well, once we narrow the field, I'd imagine we'd want to get demos scheduled and make sure we have the right folks from our side involved," I added.

"And then what?" he persisted.

"Well, then we'd want to probably look at pricing and commercial terms," I explained.

"How long do you suppose this part of the process will take?" Chuck replied.

"Somewhere between four to six weeks, I imagine," I answered.

"Great," he said, ending the exchange. "That's a lot better than, 'Got it.'"

What Chuck was teaching me was how to respond like a pro.

Let's look at another example. Let's say I send our product manager Ryan the following email:

"Hey, Ryan, I just learned that there's a new 3-D supplier talking to Macy's. I'd like to understand if this is a threat."

Ryan has several options for how to respond—most of them terrible. Here's a short list of bad responses you've probably used:

"Got it."
"No problem."
"On it."
"Sounds good."
"Will do."
"Sure thing."

Why are these answers terrible? Because Ryan has told me next to nothing about how he plans to attack this problem, how long it will take, or when I can expect answer. I am left completely in the dark with no visibility into his approach or expectation of delivery. Saying "got it" is essentially the same as saying nothing at all. No wonder Chuck was disappointed in my two-word response.

Now let's look at how Ryan could have responded to my request.

> Understood. I will prepare our standard competitive assessment, including employees, revenues, clients, products, and unique IP. I'm going to assume that you're looking for a couple-hour investment on this and that based on our learnings decide if we'd

like to dig deeper. Today is June 7; I stuck a due date for June 17 to have this completed, and I'll put thirty minutes on the calendar with you to discuss next steps.

Wow. How good did that feel, right? Clear, direct communication is like a warm, comforting blanket for your boss. I know what to expect and when to expect it. Ryan has given himself a deadline based on his workload and what makes sense for him. I have the option of accepting this or pushing for a different delivery ("Actually, I absolutely need it by June 13 for a meeting."), but the transparency means I have concrete expectations and can move on to other concerns because I know Ryan has "got it" under control.

Here is a simple outline for how you can respond like a pro:

1. Confirm your understanding of the request, especially if your boss or client isn't 100 percent clear in the request itself. Ask questions if needed, or use an example or clarify the scope to make sure you're headed on the right path. That said, it's okay to make some assumptions as you tackle the assignment. You're expected to proceed without every bit of information. Trust me, chances are quite good that the assignor doesn't have all the details either. This is your opportunity to think critically, be creative, and engage in the decision-making process with other team members.

2. Confirm ownership and others you intend to involve.

3. Confirm timing and deadlines. Don't have one? Create a deadline for when you'll know a deadline.

Training employees that are new to our organization—and even more importantly, new to the workforce—to respond like a pro is now even more important as more team members work from home. Just like the other habits we've explored, including a good personal process and effective updates through 5x5s, working from home requires that we're all better at clear and structured communication. Ambiguity and lack of ownership is much easier to creep in when we're not sitting around the same table. Learning to use the "respond like a pro" framework will help improve clarity and reduce a lot of back and forth.

Feedback Is Love: Learning to Value Constructive Criticism

My first mentor, my dad, was an accomplished high school basketball coach with a career spanning twenty years. He had a number of "coach-isms" that I remember, but the one that really (or eventually) stuck with me went something like this: "Don't worry when the coach is yelling at you. Worry when he stops, because that means he doesn't care."

Maybe because I was nine or ten at the time, it didn't sink in. Through my years as a high school baseball player and into college, I had a very difficult time taking feedback on the field. In college, this was exacerbated by my coach, Al Fulk. He could chew you a new one at the drop of a hat.

Even during my junior year as the captain of the team, he was in my face nonstop. My reaction was to get angry and set my sights on proving him wrong, hitting a thousand balls a night until my hands bled. I respected him, but I didn't love him. I hated our "feedback" sessions. I felt like I could never do anything right.

Then something happened at the end of my junior year that changed everything about my relationship with Coach Fulk. More importantly, it changed my thinking on feedback in a way that's helped me substantially in my career.

We were in the playoffs in our division, and it was a tight game going into the top of the eighth inning. I was behind the plate catching, and there was a man on second base with two outs. The batter hit a sharp line drive over the shortstop and our left fielder charged hard on the ball. He scooped it up on two hops as the runner rounded third and he fired a one-hopper to the plate. I snagged the ball and in one motion tagged the batter across the thighs. Three outs and the inning was over . . . until the ump blew the call.

We were all in disbelief. I turned to the ump and made my

case. It got heated. Then the coach from the opposing team came out of his dugout, and then Coach Fulk came running out of ours. During this heated exchange, the opposing coach directed a comment toward me. Then it happened. Suddenly, the game didn't matter. Coach Fulk looked the opposing coach in the eye and let him have it. "This is my player. Not yours. Shut the %$#@ up before I shut you up." In an instant, I saw all the immense passion and support flow out of Coach Fulk like I had never seen. Behind all of his "feedback" was a commitment to making me better. Fifteen years after I heard it for the first time, my dad's advice hit home: "Don't worry when the coach is yelling at you. Worry when he stops, because that means he doesn't care."

Feedback can be tough to internalize. It's very hard to be objective in the moment because it can feel like a personal attack. However, if you start with the fundamental belief that you're getting feedback because someone else thinks *you're worth the investment*, everything changes. This small change in perspective will help transform your career.

When it is time to provide feedback as a manager, I've learned that a very useful technique is to share a story where you've had to receive tough feedback to open the discussion. One, it humanizes you and says that you've also had to learn tough lessons. Two, it lets the person know that you're giving feedback because you're interested in her success.

REMOTE WORK AND . . . FEEDBACK IS LOVE

Implementing the "feedback is love" framework is now more important than ever. So much of a coaching session or a performance review is communicated though body language—something that is much harder to use or discern when we're not physically together. Providing constructive feedback to a team member when you've never even had lunch together is challenging. So much of coaching is based on knowing and feeling someone's intent. Using the "feedback is love" framework is an explicit way of communicating to a team member that your objective and intent is to invest in his development.

Meeting Etiquette Basics for Pros

Bosses love employees who can run effective meetings, but they *really* love employees who don't need to have meetings to be effective. Meetings are a massive time suck. I like to think of every meeting as a percentage of the day it requires. Asking for an hour meeting whether internally or with a client is like saying, "Hey, would you mind giving 12.5 percent of your day to me?" My first rule for meetings at Marxent is to never schedule a meeting for more than thirty minutes unless it is absolutely required. We practice the same with clients and sales prospects. By the way, if you're in sales, the odds that you'll get a meeting with a prospect go up by 50 percent if you ask for thirty minutes and if you don't ask for time in the morning or early in the week.

Meetings serve a vital purpose within the structure of any organization. They are an important way to organize and divide up tasks, get project feedback, and generally stay on the same page. There has been much written on how to run an effective meeting. Here are the best practices that I see put in action by the most effective employees:

1. **Never schedule same-day meetings.**

It happens. Same-day meetings need to be scheduled at times, but this should be the very rare exception. If other team members have a good personal process (see chapter 1), they have already planned their day, so taking your last-minute meeting means they need to re-plan their day. If you're constantly scheduling same-day meetings, not only do you have a planning problem, but now you're making your coworkers pay for it.

2. **Set expectations.**

Once you've determined that you do indeed need a meeting, get organized before the meeting starts by crafting a purpose (see "Carving Pumpkins and Naming Your Story" on page 67). Beyond the agenda, develop a habit of opening meetings by stating the principal objective and then asking others in the room whether they share the same expectations for the meeting. A new objective may surface, and either way you confirm that everyone knows why they are present.

3. **Follow up with owners and action items.**

If it is your meeting, you are responsible for sending out a clear email following the meeting with owners, action items, and due dates right after the meeting. I find that the best meeting follow-up isn't a long paragraph summarizing the meeting but rather a simple list of bullets organized by owners. This way your team members can easily understand their responsibilities, and you have a good structure for following up.

REMOTE WORK AND . . . MEETINGS

Good meeting etiquette is another tool in your toolbox that has become even more important when working remote. Again, remote work has created much more ambiguity in the workplace. Google Calendar has a new feature that tells me that I've spent twenty-one hours in meetings from January 10 to January 14 for an average of 8.2 hours per day. Yikes. Coordination and communication during COVID-19 have become paramount. Researchers at Harvard Business School and New York University in a December 2020 study found that "the number of meetings increased during the pandemic by 12.9 percent, on average, and the number of attendees per meeting grew by 13.5 percent." Making sure that your personal-process toolbox includes the ability to run efficient and effective meetings is now more critical than ever before.

The Need for Speed:
Advise and Move Forward [AMF]

"Advise and move forward" is one of the most powerful techniques you can employ to keep your organization moving with *speed*.

Here's a typical scenario: You have a decision that needs to be made but you think it is a decision that warrants getting your boss's approval. You put your recommendation in an email, send it off to your boss and await his or her approval. The matter is time-sensitive, and you haven't heard back in a few days, and you begin to get frustrated. If your reaction to this is, *Well, I asked and I haven't heard back*, I hate to break it to you, but this is actually *your* fault. It's your responsibility to keep the momentum. This is where the technique of "advise and move forward" is highly effective.

The practice of AMF looks like this: You provide your recommendation and then say, "If I don't hear back by end of day tomorrow, we'll need to move forward with my recommendation to keep pace on the project." This does a couple of things. First, your boss knows it is important and if a response is needed, he or she will be more likely to respond. Second, you're building trust in your judgment with your boss, colleague, or client.

Let's look at the second benefit in a bit more detail. As we explored in chapter 1 ("Developing Good Judgment"), leadership in its most basic form is making decisions. This is distinguished from management, which is providing a range of available options from which someone else has to choose. Great teams and organizations move with speed. Speed comes from trust. If you can develop your boss's or team's trust in your judgment, you can make more and faster decisions and the more you and the organization can get done. If you must wait for approval from others before you can move forward, the process and the organization is going to be slower for it.

My CMO of ten years, Sonia, taught me the value of "advise and move forward." Everyone is busy and has too much to do. And frankly, I was slow in getting back to her for one reason or another. Early in our working relationship, she started sending me emails like the following:

> We have an opportunity to participate in the Consumer Electronics Show (CES) this year. The options range from exhibiting in a 10x20 booth, sponsoring an event, etc. We have a short time to decide, as slots are being filled. My recommendation after looking at both costs and impact is that we skip the booth this year but sponsor an event. The cost to us will be $20,000. I'd like your blessing, but if I don't hear from you by Monday at 8:00 a.m., we're moving forward with my recommendation to stay on pace.

I must tell you that the first time I got an AMF from Sonia, I was a little taken aback. First, it really got my attention. I was unlikely to leave it in my email and not respond. But more importantly, I thought, *This is great, she is willing to make a decision, which is one less decision I have to make. She's a leader.* Soon, I discovered that Sonia's decision-making and judgment turned out to be sound, so it built trust. Now, I trust her judgment without hesitation and the amount of time that we need to confer on decisions is low. We simply align on our overall goals and she's off to the races. All of this creates organizational speed. And speed wins. All of this is to say, if you want to be a leader, you must do more than provide a set of options. You must make decisions. And a good way to demonstrate to your boss that you're ready to lead is to use the AMF technique to build trust.

REMOTE WORK AND ... AMF

Learning how to advise and move forward is an even more important skill to learn when working from home. One, it's a great way to reduce the overall number of communications required to make progress. Two, it is a powerful way to develop confidence in your judgment with other team members. Three, it reduces the number of meetings needed.

Good Presentation Basics: Slide Titles Should Always Be a Conclusion

Presentations are a mainstay at many jobs. There is a ton of advice out there on presentation style, format, level of detail, etc. All of that will vary based on your topic, audience, and forum. But there is one presentation habit that should always be used: the title of your slide should always be a conclusion.

What exactly does this mean? It means a title of a slide should not be a *topic* such as "Competition" or "Lead Generation" or "Hiring Priorities." Rather, the title should be a conclusion that has been reached based on the information on the slide such as, "We are behind two key competitors, but we can catch up by making one major investment," or "Lead generation costs have come down by 25 percent in the last quarter," or "Our hiring priorities are two mobile developers and a senior PM."

Think of your title as the "conclusion" or "takeaway." That is, the message that you want your audience to conclude and share with others, even if they were not present to hear your voiceover.

Why? Because you've spent hours if not days researching, internalizing, and synthesizing the materials you're presenting, and the material is probably something related to your job that you perform daily. Most of your audience is seeing this information for the first time, and they have their own responsibilities that consume their thoughts.

Your job isn't to present your recommendations piecemeal and then wait for your audience to magically reach the right conclusion. For some reason, many presenters do just this. I believe that this tendency is an attempt to "hold the floor" or perhaps to demonstrate the level of effort that went into the work. In short, get to your point as quickly as possible and then provide supporting evidence.

If the title isn't the conclusion, it should be a question. Using a question as your title is an effective way to keep the attention of your audience. Also, it immediately indicates to your audience that their input is being requested to help resolve an open issue. For example, look at the power of "How do we develop a direct selling strategy while not alienating our existing distribution partners?" versus the lackluster appeal of, say, "Direct Selling Strategy."

The Only Way to Improve Your Presentation Skills: Listen to Yourself

Being a good presenter is learned. It isn't something that comes naturally to most of us. I have learned that the only way to help someone really become a good presenter is to do what they probably fear the most—listen to themselves present. I learned this lesson from another important mentor in my life, Robert Michael Morris (his stage name), Michael, for short. Michael was my acting teacher in college. You may know him as Mickey from *The Comeback*, an HBO series starring Lisa Kudrow of *Friends* fame.

I went to college, admittedly, to play baseball and learn to become an entrepreneur. I decidedly did not go to college to participate in theater. I had never done any theater work, and frankly I had zero interest. But Michael was in desperate need for more male actors for his upcoming play. I had done a little choir to pick up a few easy credits, but I was a marginal-to-poor singer. Michael came into a choir rehearsal and made a pitch to the male members of the choir to join the cast of *The Importance of Being Earnest*. I don't remember anything about the value of being in theater from his pitch, but I do distinctly remember him saying that the ratio of women to men was something like 6 to 1. While I can't sing or act, I am decent at math. I was in.

I joined the theater troupe. As expected, I was horrible. In my inaugural debut, I played one of the title characters in Oscar Wilde's masterpiece. I did have one unintended highlight to my career that brought the house down. The line to my cousin Cecily in an attempt to woo her affections was, "Because you are like a pink rose, Cousin Cecily." Thanks to my baseball upbringing, the line came out, "Because you are like a Pete Rose, Cousin Cecily." All of which reinforced that my path was to become an entrepreneur and not an actor.

I did continue, however, to participate in many shows. And I did improve over time. With Michael's mentorship, I developed the ability to speak in public and present well. His method for helping me improve was simple: he made me listen to myself. He gave me a little voice recorder and insisted that I read my lines aloud. It had an immediate impact. I was able to hear how others heard me. I improved my pace, pronunciation, tone, and inflection. I became much more conscious of how I was actually being received versus how I thought I was being received.

I've passed on Michael's mentoring to several employees over the years who needed to develop their presentation skills.

About two out of ten took the advice; those who did changed the trajectory of their careers.

Jessi's Story

One of the employees who heeded the advice was Jessi Sparks. I've known Jessi for years and she is a dedicated and conscientious leader, but Jessi was not a good presenter. She knew her material cold, but she faced the same challenges that plague most inexperienced presenters: using lots of ums, racing through the material, talking on top of others, not allowing others to participate, and having a desperate need to get though her slides no matter the cost. Here is Jessi's story, and specifically what she learned from hearing herself.

I won't sugarcoat this; I had just given a presentation for a client, and Beck was on the call. It didn't go well. I knew it didn't go well—my heart was racing, my pulse was going a mile a minute, and honestly it felt like I was doing an impression of Sonic the Hedgehog. I braced myself for epic disapproval. But feedback from Beck was calm and steady. It started with a compliment . . . which I knew would end with "Okay Jessi, remember feedback is love."

I admit it—I don't like being criticized. I like to win and be right. But I knew this time I was all wrong and a hot mess. This time I wasn't just impacting my life, but representing my company badly, which I wanted to do my best work for. That was the bad news; the good news was the feedback I got literally changed my confidence and transformed my communication game in fourteen days.

Beck's feedback was tough to hear, but it was 100 percent true. The key word being it "was" true. Here's what he said.

1. "You say 'um' a lot . . . it's filler to hold control of the conversation. Leave room for commentary."

Ouch!

2. "You also ask double questions. Let people answer first before you pepper them with a second question. You also interrupt people. Pause and wait for a response."

Do I do that? How long have I been doing that? Crap, I just did it.

3. "You speak in one intonation, giving all words equal value. There is no hierarchy in any of your statements, which makes them all meaningless."

Hmmm . . . okay.

4. "You don't take pauses between statements. You sound like you are out of breath and are about to fall over."

5. "You are rushing—you must slow way down. Slow is smooth; smooth is fast. You need to allow others to contribute. Speak slowly and confidently. Rushing makes you seem like you are hiding something, or you are nervous. You know this content, but the truth is the customer has never seen it; let them take it in."

This isn't the first boss to point out to me rushing is sloppy, but this was the first time the criticism followed up with concrete items to help address the issues.

Then Beck gave me four tools to change these behaviors: "I want you to do something before our next meeting. I want you to run the meeting, but you need to work on some things in the next two weeks." It would have been easy for him to take over, but providing feedback and instilling confidence in me helped me realize the value I was missing out on by not learning from my mistakes.

1. **"I want you to record yourself speaking and watch it."**

What?!?!

2. **"Read out loud and notice your tone and pacing. Develop a narrative sequence with your statements. Create a story."**

I didn't quite get this one. But I asked my spouse, and he said, "Yeah, you do read at the same tone." So I asked him to help me. I read articles out loud to him, nothing special, just *New York Times* articles about the pandemic. Honestly, one was literally the latest outbreak data by state. I specifically picked data-driven statements, and then practiced changing the value of the statements with my pitch and pauses. This was a lightbulb moment for me. I was amazed how just my tone could completely change a statement for the better or worse and give it either more or less value depending on how I phrased it.

3. **"Pause and ask questions between slides."**

He went on to explain that conversation between slides is far more valuable than the slide itself. This one was an epiphany for me. You can always send the deck along after, but good questions and discussion is the equivalent of your client telling you the presentation is going well. Remember, feedback is love. That also applies in this situation, even when a client is asking challenging questions, engagement means you have their interest. That is far more important than getting through your twenty-seven-page slide deck on time. When I let go of the PowerPoint presentation as a lifeboat and embraced it as an inner tube (i.e., optional, but there just in case), it was okay that we skipped around. It was okay that we didn't get through half of it; it was just a back-up tool. The truth is you are actually the presentation, and active listening and pausing makes you 100 percent more interesting to your clients then any deck.

4. **Beck's final advice? "Spend more time practicing a confident introduction." In fact, he told me he practices this more than the whole presentation itself. I kind of think of this like sticking the landing in gymnastics.**

So that night, I admit, I cried a bit over a glass of Scotch, but then I thought, *If Beck cared enough to tell me to fix these things and still wants me to lead this presentation, I should care enough to work on myself.* So, I worked on every single suggestion, and it was career changing. Get ready to hear glass break in your own life if you take on the video challenge experiment, but it's so worth it.

Remember those extra things I mentioned I learned in addition to Beck's feedback from the video? I said "umm" seventy times in my first video. Honestly, I lost track after thirty minutes . . . it was horrifying. Apparently, I close one eye sometimes when I speak—what?! I kept scratching my neck until it turned red. Gross! Oh, and apparently in order to speak I move my hands. The videos helped me identify both positive and negative traits to reinforce my communication style. I also learned I was presenting myself as too timid and submissive with a weak voice. As a female in business, I want to present credibility and authority, but my voice and posture were contradicting what I wanted to project to the room, so I ended up sending mixed messages to my audience.

I reviewed and then I practiced, like an athlete reviewing post-game footage. I would record myself and then watch the recording, writing down negatives and positives. I did this four times, and each time I got more comfortable with the content and learned more about myself. I also re-played areas and identified places where I stumbled; this helped me identify areas to change, like modifying certain words I struggled with or how much more confident I was when I was able to use my hands. I would have never discovered any of this if I hadn't recorded myself.

I cannot explain to you how much these simple tools helped change my communication game. I still have plenty to learn, but this has shown me **feedback really is love**, and you can change anything in your communication style if you are ready to be humble, teachable, and have fourteen days of commitment.

Still not convinced if it's worth the investment? Ask Beck if he thought it was worth the effort. I know for me personally it was. The executive presentation was this morning. I killed it.

A Moonshot Habit for Your Toolbox: Listen First

In my job at Purdue's Advancement Office, I learned one more lesson that I will never, ever forget. In fact, I tell the story often when helping team members on developing their listening skills.

Chuck helped me schedule and interview for the Advance Office job just a week after we had met. I showed up early, was greeted by a receptionist, and took a seat. An elderly gentleman in his seventies, I would guess, was also in the reception area. It wasn't long before he struck up a conversation. I was a little distracted, as I was thinking about my interview, but he was very nice and engaging. I told him I was there for an interview. Then he began to ask me about my time at Purdue, what I was studying, what I hoped to do after graduation, and so on. I was happy to share my thoughts and thought I was really impressive. After about ten minutes or so of me mostly talking, Purdue's President Steven Beering walked into the reception area and said, "Neil, wonderful to see you. Welcome. Please come in."

Yeah, that Neil. *Neil freaking Armstrong*—the first man to step on the moon Neil Armstrong. I was dumbstruck. Then I thought, *Oh my god. I just met one of the most accomplished people in the history of humankind (literally), and I talked about myself nonstop.* I felt like such an idiot. I'd never forgive myself.

What I really took away from that experience was Neil Armstrong's humility. Not fake, please-ask-me-who-I-am humility, but real, genuine selflessness. I heard later that his famous quote, "One small step for man, but one giant leap for all mankind" were his words. Not something that was prepared for him by the NASA public relations team. Based on my all-too-brief encounter with him, that authenticity made sense.

The final lesson here as you develop good personal communication habits is this: if the first man on the moon can first seek to understand and learn before speaking, the rest of us mere Earth-bound mortals can do the same.

A Final Word on Good Communication Habits

I think about my moment with Dr. Armstrong often. His authenticity, warmness, and generosity were magnetic. I've seen this behavior from other highly accomplished individuals I've had the opportunity to meet.

This includes Dan Gilbert, founder of Quicken Loans, for one. Arnie Bellini, the founder of ConnectWise, is another Marxent board member, and he is exactly the same, as was Chuck Wise. They are all incredibly good at putting all of their energy into learning about the people they meet in a very genuine way. Not in that, let-me-ask-you-about-you-so-I-can-tell-you-about-me way that you've probably experienced. In fact, all of them were reticent to even talk about themselves at all. I firmly believe that this listening behavior is connected to their success.

Based on my experience with Dr. Armstrong, I built a little tool for my toolbox that I now use whenever I meet someone new, and it's something I encourage other employees to adopt. I try to ask five questions about a person's life, interests, or role before I share anything about me or the company. It's a simple technique that is actually fun and makes for much more rewarding conversations. If you're in sales, this is a great way to start building a relationship.

Whether stories are tragic (McClandless), inspiring (Armstrong), or embarrassing (Jessi, me), they are a key way that information is effectively shared *and* comprehended. It's why I'm encouraging you to frame your story and add other communication tools to your toolbox.

CHAPTER 3
GOOD PEOPLE HABITS

JEAN-PAUL SARTRE IS AN existentialist philosopher who wrote a play called *No Exit* in 1943. In the play, he depicts three characters sitting in purgatory arguing about what their final punishment will be when they get to hell. They end up trapped in this endless argument and then realize that this is it, they are *already* in hell: "So, this is hell. I'd never have believed it. You remember all we were told about the torture chambers, the fire and brimstone . . . Old wives' tales! There is no need for the red-hot pokers. HELL IS OTHER PEOPLE!"

This passage from Sartre is one of the few things I remember from philosophy class in college. I imagine if Sartre were alive today his setting for purgatory may have been an office rather than a drawing room.

While we've discussed good personal-process habits and good communication habits, perhaps the most challenging task is to navigate how to work well with the many personalities that you'll encounter in the workplace.

The first important insight in good people habits to learn is that we *all* imagine ourselves as the hero of our own story. Practicing a little self-awareness that *we* may be the "hell" that other people are experiencing is a good place to start. I promise you, that Dan the Devil's Advocate, Negative Nancy, and good old Karen at your office don't know how others are complaining about them on Slack.

For me, good communication and good personal-process habits were things I was eager to learn. I sucked at good people habits. I'm sure at many points in my career, I've been characterized by others as impatient, unempathetic, bullheaded, and arrogant. But I did learn in time with practice, coaching, and a dose of humility. Let's jump into some frameworks for good people habits, including championing strengths, weeding out toxicity, positive negotiations, the secrets of motivation, and more.

We're All Different: That's Our Strength

It's natural to gravitate in life and in work toward people that share your worldview, interests, or have similar strengths. It takes work to go out of your way to engage others where it may not feel as comfortable or natural. But different perspectives, talents, temperaments, skillsets, and styles create better teams and outcomes. Often tension between team members can be a catalyst for creativity.

A healthy and productive way to open yourself up to the habit of working well with others and seeking out other viewpoints and strengths is to first assess your own strengths (and weaknesses). Once you feel you have a good sense of your strengths, then think about what kind of people you need around you to help you address your shortcomings.

My strengths, as I've learned over the years, include the willingness to take a risk, an orientation toward action, and making difficult decisions with limited information. I'm also pretty good at taking something complex and distilling it into a simple story, which has served me well in sales. However, I'm incredibly impatient, I have to concentrate to listen sometimes, I rush everything, and I often underestimate the level of effort something might take. I've learned that I need personalities around me that are researchers and planners who can help realize important facts and identify risks. I need team members who have an aptitude to develop and maintain processes. I need technical and domain experts who can help me understand hidden complexities. I've also learned that I can be a little oblivious to others' feelings, so I need empaths on my team who are good at sensing when people need support.

Pick up the habit of actively looking for strengths and asking others what they're good at. You'll find that if you begin to focus on the strengths of others and how those strengths can be applied to help the team win, something else also happens. You stop looking for weaknesses and you have a much healthier orientation toward work and others.

There are a number of personality assessments tools in the market. The Myers-Briggs Type Indicator is one you'll often see used by larger companies. These tools are useful, but I've found them hard to apply. I think it's easier to think of personality types in the context of effective teams. The Herrmann Brain Dominance Instrument®, or HBDI, is the best example of the different types of personalities that make for a great team. And it's instantly applicable without needing a psychology degree to decipher.

Ned Herrmann headed up General Electric's Corporate University and was charged with helping teams solve problems more effectively. His Whole Brain® model is a simple four-box matrix that represents four "dominant" thinking styles. While many people may be able to operate in multiple boxes, I have found that team members seem to gravitate to one specific corner.

Herrmann's framework breaks down dominant thinking styles into four groups, each having their own color. Interestingly, the four groups aren't presented in a hierarchy. They're presented in a circle with each having equal value like the knights of the roundtable. In Herrmann's assessment, he uses colors to categorize dominant thinking styles. Here's how he frames them up:

BOX A (BLUE)

Logical, Analytical, Fact-Based, and Quantitative. Blue boxers are often mathematicians, engineers, scientists, and analysts. They're good at defining the current state and surfacing available solutions. The "What," if you will.

BOX B (GREEN)

Organized, Sequential, Planned, and Detailed. Green boxers are often project managers or may manage logistics. The "When," if you will.

BOX C (RED)

Interpersonal, Kinesthetic, Feeling-based, and Emotional. Red boxers are often teachers, HR professionals, recruiters, coaches, or trainers. The "Who," if you will.

BOX D BOX (YELLOW)

Holistic, Intuitive, Integrating, and Synthesizing. Yellow boxers are creators and decision-makers and are often leaders or entrepreneurs. The "Why," if you will.

If you stitch together a team made up of personalities from each box, you have the What (Blue), When (Green), Who (Red), and Why (Yellow) of any given topic covered. You'll have good data, you'll create a good plan, you'll have the right folks involved, and you'll have a bias toward action and decision-making—this is a great team.

What I like about the HBDI personality framework is that every type of thinking is of equal value. They're all valuable and necessary in the pursuit of solving a problem. Everyone has a place in the boat, and if all are rowing in the same direction, great things will follow.

REMOTE WORK AND . . . FINDING STRENGTHS

Getting to know your teammates in some ways became easier during the pandemic. I now spend much more face time, albeit via a screen, with employees from other offices than I ever did before. However, it is harder to assess a person's strengths without the informal communications that you get in an office environment. Therefore, adopting a toolset that allows you to pro-actively surface strengths is more important in the evolving working world. For example, team exercises like the Whole Brain® framework are effective tools for filling that gap. We're currently working on a program where we ask employees to change the background color in Zoom calls to learn more about each other during Empower Hours and other team activities.

The Personality You Don't Want in the Boat: The Machiavelli

While having diverse personality types on your team will create an effective group, there is one personality type that can be devastating to a team and even an entire organization. We'll call this person the "Machiavelli."

Niccolò di Bernardo dei Machiavelli was a senior official in the Florentine Republic. He wrote *The Prince* in 1513, which was about deception and treachery in politics. As in public life, the Machiavelli in the workplace is divisive, polarizing, and untrustworthy. The talented ones will woo you into their camp with the promise of advancement, recognition, and power. They prey on the weak-minded.

There is a performance-trust matrix that is often used in the military for evaluating candidates. Simon Sinek has a great video where he talks about the application of this matrix in the Navy SEALs.* "Nobody wants the low performer with low trust. Of course, everyone wants the high performer with high trust. What they learned is that the high-performance/low-trust person is a toxic leader and a toxic team member," Sinek observed.

This is not a new concept, but Sinek does a great job of illustrating the usefulness of this framework. Here is a simple chart that bring this framework to life:

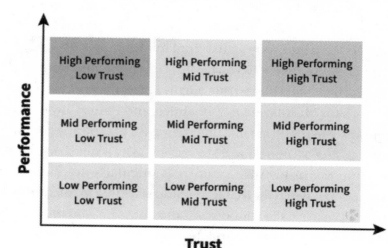

Performance vs. Trust Matrix

---

* Mike Knight, "Simon Sinek Performance vs Trust," November 10, 2019, video, 2:21, https://www.youtube.com/watch?v=kJdXjtSnZTI.

The importance of throwing high-performance/low-trust people out of the boat cannot be overstated. It literally can make or break an organization or team, and if that person is the leader of a company, it's doomed from the start.

This is a tough lesson that many leaders must learn first-hand, unfortunately. It's easy to become dependent on low-trust, talented performers. They're often great with clients, or the best salesperson, or the most talented engineer. However, the Machiavelli exhibits destructive behaviors behind the scenes that undermine trust between team members. Their goal is to consolidate power and make others and the organization dependent on them. Odds are a name or two popped in your head while reading this passage.

Remember what I said in the introduction to this book: "As a leader, your single most important responsibility will be building a strong culture." You can't do that with a Machiavelli in your midst. I'll say it again: As you become a manager and leader, the most important job you have is to keep a Machiavelli from getting into your team or organization. It is not one of the most important jobs you have; it is *the* most important job. I've learned this lesson so thoroughly in fact that our HR team screens for Machiavelli personalities, and I interview every candidate in a "culture-fit" interview with the specific goal of making sure we don't hire a Machiavelli. Why is this so incredibly important? **Because a culture is singularly determined by the worst behavior that leadership is willing to tolerate.** If a Machiavelli gets in your organization or team, you must get them out immediately, no matter how painful. If you happen to work for a Machiavelli, get out!

What does a Machiavelli look like? The following is a list of telltale behaviors. Of course, exhibiting one or two of these behaviors may not make someone a Machiavelli, but if you're checking three, four, or more off the list, your internal alarm should be going *Bing! Bing! Bing! Bing! Bing! Bing!*

- They are excellent at flattery.
- They try to control the flow of information and force their subordinates to communicate through a chain of command. They get angry if a subordinate communicates directly with leadership.
- They build coalitions and actively advocate for team members in an attempt to place allies into key roles.
- They blame others for bad news and take credit wherever they can.
- They attempt to quickly influence new team members. Who takes the new person to lunch first on your team?
- They attempt to make others dependent upon them.
- They communicate in half-truths or with partial information.
- They pit team members against each other.
- Someone must lose when they win. They are jealous and lack real generosity.

The good news is that Machiavellis are relatively easy to spot by their peers. The bad news is that leadership is usually the last to know. If you're hearing team members communicate their concerns about this type of personality, it's imperative you listen.

Strong Relationships:
Who Can You Trust When Things
Go South?

There are three types of business relationships, and this goes for relationships between companies and clients as well as relationships between teams, departments, and employees. The three types are:

1. Those that have been good so far.
2. Those that have fallen off the tracks.
3. The ones that fell off the tracks but got fixed.

The third type are your strongest and most enduring partnerships. While the first sounds the best, this type of relationship still leaves the question, "What will happen when things go south?"

Why? Because eventually everything goes south. The question is whether you're the type of company, employee, teammate, or partner that shows up to work though the challenges or you're the person who ghosts your client or team.

When things do go south, one healthy and positive way to look at the situation that has always helped me is to think, *Okay. This really sucks. But, if we can get through it, we'll have demonstrated our commitment to partnership, and they will know how we respond in a jam. Ultimately the partnership will be stronger for it.*

I've found this is a positive way to frame an issue like this with a team, as it gives them a positive outcome to look forward to if they put in the work.

Here is a simple framework for dealing with a tough situation on your way to building a positive and enduring relationship:

1. Pick up the phone. Face the situation head on. No ghosting.
2. One hundred percent transparency. Do not think your BS will fly. Give the truth and nothing but the truth.
3. Own your part of the problem. Be clear about where you can help and where you can't and need help. Avoid the blame game. It doesn't matter whose fault it is.
4. Set up regular updates to make sure everyone is current on where you stand on fixing the problem.
5. Once you've solved the problem, document how you're going to avoid it happening again.

This list is great to put in your toolbox and use whenever you find yourself in a sticky situation. I've even shared our framework with a client to communicate how we intend to respond to a challenge. I've literally sent them the list and said, "This is policy for how we deal with something we've really messed up."

I've successfully buried my worst f-ups in the deepest part

of my psyche. But just like bad situations can create great relationships, bad experiences can create useful frameworks like the one I just shared.

In 2002, Marsh Supermarkets in Indianapolis, Indiana, a one-hundred-store chain, hired us to implement their loyalty program. Kevin Bridgewater, the head of marketing at Marsh at that time is, to this day, a lifelong friend. But it wasn't always that way.

We were well into production and our system was humming along. Our software was good, but it was far from bulletproof. We were a small twenty-five-person company, but running a loyalty and promotions program for a billion-dollar retailer was a big responsibility.

Why? Because we were the folks setting up those "Buy one get one free," "Fifty cents off," and "Spend fifty dollars, get five dollars off" promotions. We were literally managing millions of dollars' worth of discounts that were being transacted every minute of every day.

One of the major limitations of their old system is that you could only set up a limited number of pre-programed offers. Our new fancy tech allowed marketers to run any number of offers that could be targeted to any person, at any time, to any store, and at any value. The downside to our tech was that you could run any promotion you wanted, which meant you needed to have a system in place to make sure every promotion was thoroughly tested. God forbid someone put five dollars off per pound of ground round rather than fifty cents off.

Yeah, that's what happened.

Even though a Marsh employee had set up the promotion, we didn't have the system in place to gut check an offer value.

We blindly sent it off to the store systems, and just like that we were giving out the richest promotion for ground round in the history of retail. Ground round was flying off the shelf. Shoppers were telling their friends. Their friends were telling their friends. So much ground round was being eaten in Indiana, the cows were getting nervous. It was a bad day.

The phone was ringing off the hook. We were all hands on deck trying to update the promotion and get it pushed to stores as quickly as possible. We finally did get it fixed, but the damage had been done. We'd given out more discounts than we would make in software fees for the next few years.

We had a wonderful relationship with the Marsh leadership team up until this point. But now the relationship would be tested. All sorts of thoughts entered our minds as to how we would address the situation. Blame the employee? Consult our contract to look at our legal obligations? Even perhaps just hide under a rock.

In the end, we fell on our swords, owned up to our responsibilities, and went to work to solve the problem while actively communicating our progress. Once solved, we put a plan together immediately to demonstrate how it would never happen again. In the end, Kevin and Marsh appreciated our ownership of the problem, transparency, and our all-hands-on-deck response. That bad experience, in the end, communicated to Marsh how we would respond in a bad situation, and we earned their respect as well as a long-term partner.

I can tell you something else: nobody shopped Kroger for a few days.

REMOTE WORK AND ... STRONG RELATIONSHIPS

Building strong relationships in a post-pandemic world is exceedingly more difficult. Earlier this year we signed a new client in New Zealand. We went through the entire sales process completely remotely, something that I had never experienced with such a large multibillion-dollar company. Our software for them wouldn't just be a nice-to-have, it would be the principal tool that store associates would use to do their jobs every day. There would be no way to drop everything and go on site to demonstrate to them that we were all hands on deck if we had any major problems. Moreover, we shared literally no overlapping work hours. So how do you build confidence and trust? Our solution was to be proactive with them and share our problem-solving framework as a way of forecasting to them how we address problems when (not if) they do go south. This simple technique demonstrated how we value our partners and ultimately helped us to win the deal.

Never Negotiate on Gratitude

Negotiating is a part of nearly every job. We negotiate when we're applying for a new job or want a promotion. We negotiate with prospective clients during the sales process. We negotiate with clients about deliverables and due dates. We negotiate with bosses for resources. We're constantly negotiating.

I've been head-to-head with some tough negotiators, and I've witnessed great negotiators in action. There are numerous books on the subject, but I've learned one undeniable truth that should be at the center of every negotiation: never negotiate on gratitude.

There is a great book by Robert Greene called *The 48 Laws of Power*, which is filled with great lessons and cautionary tales. The thirteenth law in the book is titled "Appeal to People's Self Interest, Never to Their Mercy." The general gist of the lesson is "never negotiate on gratitude." Greene tells the story of Stefano di Poggio, Castruccio Castracani, and a fourteenth-century Italian conflict to make his point, but I'll simplify it for our purposes here—although let's keep the fourteenth-century theme for fun.

Let's imagine that you are the king or queen of the eastern part of a continent that has water access. You have a counterpart who is the king of the western part of the continent that also has water access. Between you and your western peer is the largest and most powerful kingdom, which sits in the center of the continent. The largest and most powerful "middle" kingdom doesn't have water access and would like to because trade and shipping is becoming an increasingly important commercial asset.

Now, imagine the middle king comes to you and says, "Good day, Eastern King, I'd like to partner with you or the Western Kingdom to build the most powerful trading route on the continent. Why should I work with you?"

If focused on your prior contributions, your pitch might look something like this: "Well, Middle King, we've been friends for many years, I've defended your borders. We helped you out during the great drought. I've paid my taxes regularly, and your daughter married my son. Pick me!"

Middle King says, "Thank you very much," and rides off on his horse to the Western Kingdom. Upon arrival, the Middle King says, "Good day Western King. I'd like to partner with you or the Eastern Kingdom to build the most powerful trading route on the continent. Why should I work with you?"

The Western King says, "Look, we've had our differences. I haven't defended your borders well. We didn't pitch in during the great drought. I'm always late on my taxes, and my daughter thinks your son is ugly. But, if you pick me, I'll get rid of the competition for you."

Guess who Middle King picked?

The lesson here is that when you negotiate on gratitude, you're making the other person feel indebted to you (i.e., "You owe me."). Nobody likes to feel indebted, and in every relationship, there are two sides to every story. While you may think that by reeling off all the historical reasons why you've earned someone's gratitude and loyalty, the other person is thinking, *Geez, didn't I give you this job and provide you this training and give you these opportunities?*

In practice, this happens nearly every time someone asks for a raise or promotion: "Look what I've done for you; you owe me." While you think you're listing your merits, no matter how grand, that may not be how your ask is being received. Don't be the Eastern King. Focus on the future.

Let's look at a few practical examples that you're likely to encounter in your career and how you can focus the conversion to make it future oriented.

You have a client contract that is coming up for renewal. Your solutions have performed well over the last two years. If your approach is to list out how your product has performed, the client is probably thinking, *Well yeah, but my team has also invested significantly in driving that performance.* A much better approach would be to focus on your product roadmap and the benefits to the client in the future—a topic where you can generate excitement and future opportunity.

- You've worked hard and you want a promotion. Rather than listing all your accomplishments and why you "deserve" the opportunity, build a ninety-day plan and focus on the future value of your contributions.
- You need more people and financial resources for a project you're recommending. Rather than focus on the

resources that other projects have gotten or how your department has been underfunded, focus on the future value your project can create for the business.

In every instance, focusing on the future benefit is a topic both parties can easily agree on. The tenor of the conversation becomes collaborative rather than adversarial, and there is no judgment about which party is deserving of past credit.

Carry Your Own Stress

Mark Cuban has a widely read piece on CNBC about his favorite type of employees—those who reduce his stress. His point was that if he has someone on his team who reduces his stress, he is never letting them go. Let's talk a bit about carrying your own stress and why this is a great tool to have in your people toolbox.

I think it's safe to say that everyone is stressed out, overworked, and juggling lots of plates. You're not unique or special. Your boss probably already knows this as well. Guess what, your boss is probably carrying a tremendous amount of stress too.

My brother, Barry, has been my partner for many years. He runs Product, Engineering, and Operations. I run Sales, Marketing, and Finance. Basically, he runs one half of the company, and I run the other. We have one very important rule that we always adhere to—you carry your stress and I carry mine.

Asking Barry to worry about whether we're going to close a round of financing we need to sustain the business while he must get an application in market in the next fifteen days is unreasonable. Likewise, he can't give me his delivery stress at the same time I'm trying to negotiate a very important deal. Now and again, we break that rule, but only when I know he is in a low-stress moment and need his counsel.

Team members that find it necessary to constantly communicate how hard they are working, how many roadblocks they've had, how many customer issues there have been, how many hours they've put in, and so forth often think that their frenetic communication style is making a good impression. Now, everyone needs support now and again. I need to blow off steam too once in a while, but if you're chronically sharing your stress with everyone around you, it's just not a sustainable, helpful, or professional scenario.

Understanding that everyone is under pressure and having the professional maturity to carry your own stress takes some learning. I must confess that I was guilty of this behavior early in my career. While I thought I was demonstrating dedication, commitment, and work ethic, I'm sure it wasn't being viewed in that light. I looked out of control, messy, hurried, frantic, and overwhelmed.

If you can muster the self-control to carry your own stress, as Mark Cuban said, the benefits are enormous, as your boss will never ever want to let you go. Is it easy? Of course not. But the first thing that may be helpful to understand is that you're not alone. Everyone, or at least most everyone, feels the same. And your boss likely already knows the job isn't easy.

I've learned that the psychological term for this behavior is called "trauma dumping." According to a 2021 *Psychology Today* article, trauma dumping is the term used to describe intense oversharing, which can leave everyone involved feeling more distressed and helpless. People who trauma dump find it hard to process, filter, and regulate emotions, especially when stressed. Odds are that you've worked with someone guilty of this behavior. It's exhausting, and in most cases, it's chronic.

I've counseled many employees on how to manage their own stress. To be clear, I'm not talking about employees who are dealing with mental health issues or another personal crisis. Addressing these situations is of course a whole other matter requiring HR intervention and professional counseling. Here I'm talking about the day-to-day stress that comes with every job. Here are some useful tools to help you avoid the "chicken little" label:

1. Don't email or Slack your issues in a one-off, ad hoc way. Frame up the issue or issues, come up with some suggestions, and schedule a dedicated time to run though issues.
2. Take a minute to collect yourself and your thoughts before you pull the trigger. Give yourself some time to get some perspective. Responding in the moment is always less than optimal.

3. Find a stress buddy. Perhaps this can be a peer in your organization who can lend an ear and offer up some creative ideas.
4. Write out your thoughts. Just the discipline of framing up your thoughts is a good exercise to help work through an issue.
5. Google your situation and look for tools or frameworks that you might use to solve a problem.

Experience will also give your more and more confidence in dealing with stressful situations. Patterns will emerge and you'll be able to put a situation you've seen before in the right context.

REMOTE WORK AND . . . SHARING STRESS

Slack is equally a lifeline for connectivity and sharing *and* a constant source of annoyance for most of us. If it wasn't so before, in a pandemic world, chat tools have become the predominant way we all communicate now. While a great resource, ad hoc communications can be incredibly randomizing. The ability to stay focused on writing a document or developing code can be and is often interrupted with the constant ping of new messages. And the informality of it makes it much too easy to overshare or blow off steam. Showing discipline in your communications is, now more than ever, an important skill to master.

Feedback and Motivation

It is super easy to demotivate someone. This one took me a bit of time to learn. You can spend years building up a really positive and motivated employee or teammate only to pay the price when you are overly critical . . . Or worse, you might embarrass or ridicule someone in front of their peers.

Coaches, including my dad, are fond of saying that not all players respond to feedback in the same way. Some players are more likely to respond to encouragement, while others need to be challenged. In general terms, this is positive versus negative reinforcement. Some argue that each is useful at different times and depending on the situation. Goals and incentives are also other dimensions that comingle with the effectiveness of feedback. But whether positive or negative feedback is being used, *what's* said and *how* it's said carry equal weight. And sometimes, I've learned, the best thing is to say nothing at all.

I had this super smart employee, Darren, who worked for me for several years. He worked in product development and his work was incredibly thorough. I actually loved receiving and reviewing his work. For the first several exchanges, I would go through his presentations and make comments and suggestions and ask questions. I thought I was actively participating and showing him that I took great care in reviewing his work, which was always A+. But no matter what I did, he'd go into a funk for two weeks with the slightest bit of feedback.

Finally, having somewhat given up and wanting to avoid conflict I just wrote back, "Perfect, no changes." And voilà! I found the key to motivating Darren. His energy grew. So did his confidence and our partnership. I learned that sometimes telling someone "perfect"—even if I have minor thoughts—is much more motivating and drives increased performance than being nitpicky, especially when the feedback is on the margins. The learning for me here was that instilling confidence and motivation are much more important than perfection.

Another element of a good feedback framework is the use of stories. I learned this from my first mentor, Chuck Wise. Chuck was a story machine. He had this wonderful way of providing feedback that was so humble and unassuming that you'd learn a lesson and walk away feeling inspired rather than disheartened. He would simply tell me a story. I swear he had a story for every situation. Sometimes the story was about his own experience. Other times it was a story about someone he knew or something he read. I wouldn't be surprised if some of his stories were completely made up. But it didn't matter, as they always did the trick. Chuck's best stories were about his own learning experiences. They humanized him and made me feel like what I needed to learn was something that everybody needed to learn. It was normal. I wasn't deficient in some way; I just needed to learn it too.

Here's a good list of frameworks for productive ways to deliver constructive feedback while reinforcing employee morale and keeping folks motivated:

1. Communicate that "feedback is love" as you open the conversation (full lesson in chapter 2 on page 76). In short, you're providing feedback because you think someone is worth the investment.
2. Use stories to communicate that everyone had to learn at one point. Be clear that they are not being singled out or deficient.
3. First ask someone what they already learned and what they would do differently before you provide direct feedback. I often find that the lesson has already been learned.
4. Ask, "Who do you think does this well?" Then pair them up for a peer-to-peer learning session.

5. Focus the conversation on desired outcomes and goals versus behavior. Then use the discussion to surface what activities might produce the desired results.

When You're Really Not Hanging in There

Why are we motivated? How and why do people get demotivated? If you're demotivated or you have a demotivated person on your team, what can you do to turn it around?

I remember seeing an HR poster in an office that read, "Your altitude is determined by our attitude." I think it was right next to a poster of a cat hanging from a tree branch that read, "Hang in there." Both, in my view, are pretty worthless platitudes. Yes, of course having a positive attitude is helpful, but motivation isn't just about a good outlook on life; it lives much deeper in our psyche. Rather, motivation is driven by a number of interacting variables or conditions that must resonate with someone. Moreover, not all of us are motivated in exactly the same way.

I've nearly always felt motivated and never imagined that would change . . . until it did. And when it did, I had one heck of a time self-diagnosing. Worse, up until I experienced it myself, I was very quick to judge someone if they were not motivated, chalking it up to a character flaw or bad attitude. My own situation sent me on a path of self-discovery that not only helped me understand my own issues but shed new light on how I viewed the lack of motivation in others.

After our first startup had sold to NCR, I spent three great years there learning to operate within a much larger organization. However, I was shocked at the sheer number of people that seemed demotivated or just did the minimum. It was so prevalent that when you'd meet someone that was really motivated and loved their job, it stood out. I really didn't understand it and sort of just assumed that this is what happens as organizations get large and people feel like a small cog in a big machine.

After my stint at NCR, I joined a firm called Catalina Marketing. You know Catalina. They're the folks that distribute coupons at the checkout based on your purchasing behavior. Catalina had been a public company for a number of years, but their growth had slowed. They were acquired and taken public by a private equity company. This new owner infused the business with new cash and was pushing for growth and innovation. I was hired to help contribute to Catalina's innovation efforts and it was extremely exciting. Moreover, while much of the economy was suffering from the housing and mortgage crisis starting in 2007, Catalina was growing faster than ever as brands were investing heavily in coupons and promotions to win over shoppers. It was a great place to be.

One of the initiatives that I had the opportunity to help lead was the development of Catalina's digital business. Smartphones were still relatively new, and there were all sorts of imaginative things you might do. You could now deliver coupons to consumers on the go, and they could redeem offers by scanning barcodes with their phone's camera. I was highly motivated by the newness of it all and the unlimited possibilities.

We assembled a great team and hired some external experts to help us, and we built an exciting plan to take on the space over the next several months. We worked insane hours with all of the energy of a startup but with the resources of a several hundred-million-dollar company. We wrapped up the plan in time for a board meeting in New York, and I was ready to pitch. I had never been in a board meeting like that before, and I was nervous like a schoolboy but champing at the bit. The meeting went well, and the room was buzzing. Then someone from the board said, "This is great. Who are we going to get to run this thing?" My heart sank. It had never occurred to me that all this work wasn't an audition for the role. I was instantly demotivated.

In retrospect, what I felt was silly and juvenile. I was going to be part of the team and that was still amazing. In fact, they asked me to run the search for a leader and that leader would ultimately report to me. But damn it, I didn't want to manage someone who was going to do it. I wanted to do it, and it ate at me. Anyone looking at the situation from the outside would have for sure looked at me like I was an idiot if I had shared my feelings, but the feelings were there nevertheless, and I just couldn't shake it. I kept talking to myself to try and make sense of it and get myself out of the funk, but I just couldn't . . . for months. It made no earthly sense to feel so demotivated.

During my funk I started to research motivation to try and figure out what the hell was going on with me. In the end, I realized that I simply felt underappreciated and unrecognized.

While feeling underappreciated is one reason a team member might feel unmotivated, I've learned there are several other important contributors to motivation. Whether you yourself are struggling with lack of motivation or you need to help someone else with recapturing their motivation, here is a helpful framework for the most common things to consider. I think that, as you read though this list, it is helpful to put yourself on both sides of the table.

- *Incentives:* Incentives like compensation, bonuses, and vacation time are givens and important to get right. They need to be clearly communicated and consistent. Nothing is more demotivating to employees if they feel like compensation is unclear or might change unexpectedly. Make sure to get these right and make sure they are consistent.

- *Appreciation:* I've come to believe that a simple "thank you" and show of appreciation goes a long way. It's easy to do and doesn't cost you anything. It works great both with team members and clients. I believe that it is so powerful that I start and end nearly every single communication with it.

- *Recognition and Visibility:* Public recognition is another easy one that can be very meaningful to team members. Take time during team events to have a special session where individuals are recognized for their contributions.

- *Control:* There is little worse in a job than not having a say in how you accomplish your work. Don't micromanage. Give direction based on the outcomes that you need to achieve, and give enough room for team members to give input on how to get there.

- *Community:* Humans are animals that survive as members

of a tribe. Tribeless humans are unhappy and scared. We need to belong to a group that has shared interests. We need to be with a group where we feel protected. We also love to feel a part of something that has meaning and that contributes to a greater good. Make sure the organization has a defined purpose and allow room for leaders of teams to create their own team values and culture. Make sure the organization has a place in the community through both providing jobs and giving back to important causes.

- **Competency:** This one is particularly interesting. I've learned that what we thought was a disgruntled team member was just someone who didn't feel good at their job and he or she was worried about failing or being found out. Make sure to provide proper training and education opportunities. Connect less experienced team members to mentors that they can go to for guidance and support.

REMOTE WORK AND ... MOTIVATION

While all are important, one of the motivation variables we discussed in this section has become more important for remote team members: community. In an office environment, creating a sense of community for a team happens somewhat organically. But in a post-pandemic world, teams and organizations must be much more intentional and have a system to make sure community is built and maintained. We'll talk about this more in the next section as we explore good culture habits. For instance, building community around what your organization cares about, such as a local charity (e.g., team activities for the local Habitat for Humanity), now must become a decentralized exercise. To accomplish this, we launched a Community Spotlight LinkedIn campaign where we feature employees and the charitable organizations that they support. Great companies should stand for something beyond their own products or services; this is an important part of community building.

A Final Word on Good People Habits

Learning to effectively connect with other people is a critical part of your good work habits toolbox. Here we've explored four of the most important people habits that are the most common topics on which I have team members seeking advice and counsel: building good teams, developing good relationships, dealing with a destructive team member, and instilling motivation. Adding these frameworks to your toolbox will make you a stronger contributor and a capable team member, manager, or leader. No matter what your role, when your toolbox starts to fill up, you are in an ideal position to positively influence the culture of your organization. Whether that culture is already well established and you're maintaining a tradition worth being proud of or it's still evolving and you're helping to build and carry out the vision, this is an exciting place to be . . . which leads us to chapter 4.

CHAPTER 4
GOOD CULTURE HABITS

I'VE HAD THE OPPORTUNITY to see business through the lens of a startup during the dot-com boom; a six-billion-dollar, hundred-year-old public company; a company transition from being public to private; and a company at the forefront of virtual worlds. The immutable truth regardless of technology or business trends or the size and maturity of a company is that good work habits are a critical part of any winning strategy. And this is as true for the individual as it is for the team and an organization.

Culture Systems

We create good systems and processes in an organization to help it run more efficiently and effectively. These systems and processes are really just team or company habits where everyone understands their respective roles. Organizations spend millions and billions of dollars to make sure systems are well defined and that employees are trained to operate within these systems.

Whether you're an individual contributor, manager, or leader, we all know and feel that one of the most important drivers of success is the culture of an organization. When a team or company lacks a good culture, it's like a stench in the air that everyone can smell but nobody can quite figure out where it's coming from (and even when you know it's coming from the Machiavelli, if no one takes away the toxicity, the company will continue to struggle).

Culture is a major topic today in every company no matter how big or how small. Now it's touted as *the* most important thing in the long-term success of any organization, as it drives recruiting, retention, and performance. But how do you contribute to and build a great culture? And, if it's so important, how does it translate into a competitive differentiator for your team or organization?

While the first three chapters have been dedicated to good *individual* work habits, this chapter is dedicated to those who are or aspire to be managers and leaders. As we talked about in the introduction, if you build a good work habits toolbox of your own and help others on their journey, it is inevitable that leadership opportunities will follow.

I've come to believe that without question, building your team's or company's cultural habits is the most powerful competitive weapon in your arsenal. But how do you build a great culture? First, it is important to understand what isn't culture building.

Culture Isn't Principles

Many organizations confuse company principles with company culture. Here is a fun list of company principles from some of the most well-known companies in the world, including IKEA, Coca-Cola, Google, Facebook, Kellogg's, Nike, Proctor & Gamble, Southwest Airlines, Starbucks, Twitter, and Zappos.

- "You get what you inspect, not what you expect."
- "You can't manage what you don't measure."
- "Stewardship, integrity, respect for the individual."
- "Passion is the heart of our company. We are continuously moving forward, innovating, and improving."
- "Customer commitment, quality, integrity, etc."
- "Respect, empathy, responsibility, etc."
- "We strive to create economic opportunities for those who have been denied them and to advance new models of economic justice that are sustainable and replicable."
- "The courage to shape a better future; commitment in heart and mind."
- "Focus on impact, move fast, be bold . . ."
- "Passion means we use our drive and commitment to energize, engage, and inspire others."
- "Do the right thing."

These principled statements are great. Everyone should aspire to realize these behavioral principles, but *principles* do not make a *culture*. I've come to learn that having a good culture is not all that different from having good personal-process habits, good communication habits, or good people habits.

Culture must also be a *habit*. But rather than being a personal habit, it has to be a shared set of habits across a team or organization. Further, these shared cultural habits must be unique to your organization and contribute directly to what helps a company be great and win. We seek to demonstrate this every day at Marxent.

Four Steps to Building Good Culture Habits

A good culture is the result, not the "input" or "activity." We've learned that the key to a good culture is *what the team believes will help us win if we repeatedly do it together.* At its most basic level, company culture is a shared habit.

Step 1 in building good culture habits is deciding what habits help you win. Step 2 is building team habits. Step 3 is reinforcing and rewarding team habits. Step 4 is hiring for team habits. Let's look at each step in more detail.

STEP 1: DECIDING WHAT HELPS YOU WIN

The first step is to give considered thought to what specific behaviors will help you work together and win. They must be clear, easily understood, repeatedly actionable, and rewarded. While there is no set number, I think that a small number of three to five shared company habits is much more effective than a long list.

When Marxent went in search of what helped us win, we focused internally on our best team members. Odds are you'll find your shared habits right in front of you. They're living proof of the habits you seek. All you need to do is amplify them.

Here are the four shared habits we landed on at Marxent and why. Beyond just naming the habit, a clear statement of "why" is critical.

1. **Consistency:** We operate in a fast-growing space with large competitors. Moreover, many more startups are entering the space all the time. It's imperative that we move quickly and decisively, and that team leaders and individuals can be trusted. As we deconstructed what leads to speed, we surmised that our best performers had built up high levels of trust, which leads to less oversight and micromanagement. Where did that trust come from? It wasn't a feeling or some intuition. It came from the fact that they have great personal processes and are highly consistent. That is, *consistency* creates trust, and that trust translates to speed.

2. **Grit:** The second behavior we observed in our best performers and team was grit—the ability to stay focused day after day on long-term goals and to believe there was a way to solve a problem. If the front door was closed, they try the window or the back door. If those were locked, it was time to break out the sledgehammers or shovels and find a way through or under. This never-say-die approach and self-reliance was helping us solve challenging and thorny problems again and again.

3. **Generosity:** The third behavior that we observed in our top performers was a generosity toward their teammates. This comes through in genuine celebration when others did well, had a big win, or got promoted, and a real appreciation for the contributions of others. Teammates that know they were valued and appreciated are much

less likely to want to leave, which leads to retention and continuity in the business.

4. **Build Others Up:** The fourth behavior we observed that helped us win is what my father and basketball coach called "point guard behavior." That is the willingness to assist others and help them succeed. Needless to say, this leads to the team succeeding too. A team full of proactive teachers and mentors accelerates onboarding and professional development.

These are Marxent's shared winning habits. What habits do you want to prioritize in your organization?

STEP 2: BUILDING TEAM HABITS

Once you've identified what behaviors you believe will help you win, the next step is to build shared habits that directly reflect and reinforce this behavior: a symbol, if you will. We have learned that there doesn't need to be a lot of them. In fact, one or two really good ones are more effective and easier to maintain.

1. **Consistency Habits:** We reviewed 5x5s earlier as a great tool under personal-process habits as a way to demonstrate to your boss that you have the consistency gene. To reinforce this message, we require that all employees provide a 5x5 every week. We provide a sample of a good 5x5 to all new hires as part of onboarding training. 5x5s have become a way of life and serve as simple but very tangible evidence that an employee has bought into the value of consistency. We speak to the importance of the 5x5 at all team events and course-correct with employees who fall off the bandwagon. We also require attendance at daily standups and all-team meetings.

2. **Grit:** Telling someone they exhibited grit is among the highest compliments you can give someone at Marxent. When we find examples of employees exhibiting grit, we celebrate it with gusto. We have a shared Slack channel where employees are recognized by other employees are recognized for heroic stories of grit. Here's an actual example.

3. **Generosity:** Generosity in its simplest form is saying "thank you" or "congratulations" to those who are deserving. Nothing builds team happiness and camaraderie more than simply feeling appreciated. Our shared habit for generosity is a biweekly all-team meeting that is dedicated to saying thank you. While we accomplish other objectives on this meeting as well, a collective show of generosity is the main goal. Each team member shares a "top" of the week, which is something they accomplished, and then gives a "shout out" to the person or persons that helped them. It's so simple, and what's interesting is that once in place, a ritual like this is self-sustaining. New team members listen to existing team members and simply pattern their behavior. Each "shout out" reinforces that it takes all of us to win.

4. **Build Others Up:** Much like grit, being credited with training another team member or helping another team member solve a problem is held in the highest

esteem. Again, we use a Slack channel to share stories and celebrate these individuals.

That's it. Not all that complicated or difficult. But the power doesn't lie in the single act; it embedded in the hundreds and thousands of individual statements and reinforcements of consistency, grit, generosity, and helping others.

STEP 3: REINFORCING AND REWARDING TEAM HABITS

The third component to building shared habits is visibility, reinforcement, and recognition. We accomplish this in several forums, including:

1. Reviewing our values and habits in the strategic plan every year.
2. Reviewing our shared habits every quarter when we review team and company performance.
3. Handing out Consistency, Grit, Generosity, and Build Others Up awards each quarter by taking nominations from the team.
4. Posting an employee spotlight on LinkedIn every two weeks that features an employee and how they exhibit one of our four team habits.

HERE ARE SOME ACTUAL EXAMPLES OF EMPLOYEE SPOTLIGHTS:

While not intended, these employee spotlights have turned out to be a fantastic recruiting tool. Prospective employees regularly comment on the fact that employees are so prominently featured and recognized. This program also grew into a series of community spotlights that feature team members contributing to various charities:

SUPPORTING OUR
COMMUNITIES

MARXENT

Noelle Baus, Saundra Baughman,
& Sarah Geehan

Senior Quality Assurance Analyst, Senior
Quality Assurance Analyst, & Product Manager
Dayton, OH

"Leadership allots time
for us to volunteer to
causes we care about."

SUPPORTING OUR
COMMUNITIES

MARXENT
3D COMMERCE

STEP 4: HIRING FOR HABITS

Our final commitment to our shared values and habits is that we hire for them. That is, we actively screen candidates during the hiring process to assess if they already exhibit these behaviors. We ask for and look for examples where they've demonstrated these behaviors in prior roles. And before any hire is made, we're explicit about our commitment to these values and directly ask candidates if they are committed to participating in these habits with us. The result of these conversations in nearly all cases is excitement to join an organization that is so explicit about what we value.

Remote Work Revolution: Working from Home Together

Sometimes I feel like I was fortunate enough to be born at just the right time. I was graduating college in 1993 just as the personal computer was entering homes. Email became a thing just as I started graduate school in 1994. Amazon was founded the same year. Netscape allowed us to browse the Internet soon after. I remember trying to explain how hyperlinks worked to my coworkers with marginal success. Then I got to be a part of the dot-com boom (and bust) in the early 2000s. Desktops became laptops. Single board computers introduced tablets shortly thereafter. Then Razr phones (how cool where those?), then the first really bad smartphones that didn't sync to anything. Then in 2007 we had the first iPhone. Facebook got popular somewhere in there as well (hey, not everything can be perfect). Then in 2011, 3D tech in applications other than gaming became possible. (Little known fact, Barry wrote the very first augmented reality application for the app store in 2011.) Virtual reality soon followed. And now I find myself part of something called the Metaverse. I can't imagine a much better thirty-year stretch than that to be in business.

Developing good personal-process, communications, and good people habits, as we've explored, are now more important than ever. Moreover, the intentional building of shared culture habits is just as important. Remote work, which was ignored or disparaged by many organizations for years, is now a force to stay. It's illuminating the importance of these disciplines. To ignore that is to hurt yourself as a contributor and as a leader in your organization.

As mentioned at the opening of this book, good work habits are even more important to teach and reinforce for employers, especially for employees that are brand new to the workforce. This is much more difficult to do without a physical work environment.

I suspect that teaching and reinforcing good work habits and building good culture habits for remote teams will become a much researched and examined area of academic study. While good work habits are not part of the educational curriculum today nor an often-taught discipline in most organizations, I believe that COVID-19 will be the catalyst.

Today we're living in a world in transition between the old ways of working and a future where billion-dollar companies will be built entirely by remote workforces.

From the personal computer, to email, to the Internet, to mobile phones, to social media, to virtual reality, we've been witness to some of the most transformational technologies in the history of mankind over the last twenty-five years. They've all transformed the way we live and work. But nothing will be more transformative than our new remote work reality. And its success, exhibited in those first billion-dollar remote unicorns, will need to be built on a solid foundation of good work habits and teams that come together and win with great culture habits.

ABOUT THE AUTHOR

From being founding CEO at a tech startup in the early days of the internet browser that was acquired by a multinational Fortune 500 company, to heading innovation for a public company transitioning to the private sector, to founding another tech startup at the forefront of augmented and virtual reality, Beck Besecker has worked with companies at all stages of growth and managed thousands of employees. He believes creating jobs is among the highest of callings, as jobs give purpose and meaning, allow people to support their families, and, if done well, create a virtuous circle of development and mentorship that keeps our communities and country thriving. Beck grew up as a farmer in Darke County, Ohio, and is blessed with a strong work ethic, supportive family, and entrepreneurial spirit.